Join the RichClub

How to enrich your life & the lives of others

PETER SWITZER

RUSSH

Media + Publishing

London   Sydney   New York

First published in 2019 by RUSSH Media + Publishing Pty Ltd
Level 4, 10 Spring St, Sydney NSW 2000

The moral rights of the author have been asserted

Creator:	Switzer, Peter - Author
Tittle:	Join The Rich Club: How to enrich your life and the lives of others/Peter Switzer
ISBN:	978-0-6485511-0-2 (pbk.)
Notes:	Includes glossary
Subjects:	Finance, Personal, Savings and investments - Australian - Handbooks, manuals, etc.

Managing Editor, Maureen Jordan
Cover design by Thea McLachlan
Cover image by Andre Chan & Thea McLachlan

The author and publisher would like to thank the following copyright holders, organisations and individuals for their permission to reproduce copyright material in this book: Bourse Communications, Chantwest, SuperRatings, Andex Charts Pty Ltd/Vanguard Investments Australia Ltd.

Copyright © Peter Switzer

Printed in Australia SOS Print + Media Group (Aust) Pty Ltd

Disclaimer
The material in this publication is of the nature of general comment only, and does not represent professional advice. It is not intended to prove specific guidance for particular circumstances and it should not be relied on as the basis for any decision to take action or not take action on any matter which it covers. Readers should obtain professional advice where appropriate, before making any such decision. To the maximum extent permitted by law, the author and publisher disclaim all responsibility and liability to any person, arising directly or indirectly from any person taking or not taking action based on the information in this publication.

The author is not affiliated with and does not endorse any of the corporate entities mentioned in or involved in the distribution of this work, or any third party entities whose trade marks and logos may appear on this work.

Switzer Financial Group
Australian Financial Services Licence 286531

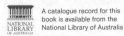

A catalogue record for this book is available from the National Library of Australia

"Apart from being a well-educated and highly experienced finance industry expert, Peter perceives market gaps and is always looking for where the opportunities are. Once identified, he has this ability to execute with a rare combination of energy and focus, coupled with reading a market and nailing the solution to that market. Rare indeed."

Mark Bouris, founder of Wizard, Yellow Brick Road and host of *The Apprentice*.

"Peter Switzer is the most honest and reliable finance guy in the country."

Gerry Harvey, Chairman, Harvey Norman.

"Peter's gifts are his grasp of money matters and his ability to make them understandable to others."

Alan Jones, Radio Broadcaster, Macquarie Media.

"Peter Switzer is one of Australia's great communicators when it comes to all things financial. His no nonsense, direct and entertaining style is not only informative but interesting. For that reason alone *Join the Rich Club* is a great read."

Sir John Key, GNZM AC Prime Minister NZ (2008-2016).

"Peter and I talked money for years on ABC radio. If only I'd listened to what he was saying, I'd be rich!"

James Valentine, Radio Host, ABC Radio 702.

To Maureen,
For richer, for poorer...

CONTENTS

ICONS USED IN THIS BOOK

This symbol appears next to words of advice that are highly enlightening!

This symbol appears next to terms that are more difficult to explain and need further research.

This symbol appears next to text that should be read with caution.

This symbol appears next to words of advice that Peter makes loud and clear.

This symbol appears next to words of advice you should write down.

This symbol appears next to words of advice worth committing to memory!

"Give someone $20 and you feed them for a day. Teach someone how to make money and you feed them for a lifetime."

Chinese Proverb adapted by Peter Switzer for *Join the Rich Club*

My thanks…

To Maureen Jordan, my business partner, for always making my work more readable and understandable. And to my business partner and friend, Paul Rickard, whose technical expertise keeps me balanced. My sincere thanks to Renee Switzer for her professionalism and diligence. To Thea McLachlan, who worked tirelessly on this book. And the entire Switzer team who are always "ready aye ready" to lend a hand. I hope the end result is that they become rich!

*"When I started counting my blessings,
my whole life turned around."*

Willie Nelson, US songwriter

ABOUT THE AUTHOR

Peter Switzer is one of Australia's leading business and finance commentators. The son of a small business owner determined to see his son educated at university, Peter started his career as a secondary school teacher at his alma mater, Waverley College in Sydney's eastern suburbs. He completed his Master of Commerce during this time, leaving Waverley to teach at Sydney Grammar School, after he returned from a two-year stint living in London. Peter began his PhD at the University of New South Wales with a view to becoming an academic but realised early in the piece that his destiny was talking to larger crowds. He kicked off a career in the media, writing for News Corporation newspapers, as well as working with the outrageously popular Doug Mulray and The D-Generation for the Triple M network for a number of years during radio's halcyon days.

Peter hosted the inflight entertainment business programme on Qantas called Talking Business, for 10 years. His foray into TV began with Clive Robertson's Newsworld on the Seven Network. Later he hosted the popular Switzer programme on the Sky News Business Channel for a decade. This programme now screens on YouTube and www.switzer.com.au. Nowadays he's a regular commentator on money and business on radio stations 2GB (Sydney), 4BC (Brisbane), 3AW (Melbourne), 2CC (Canberra), 6PR (Perth) and ABC (Adelaide).

Peter started Switzer Media + Publishing in 1983 with his wife Maureen. Over the years the business developed into a full suite of financial services business, built off Peter's reputation for trusted, open communication and knowledge. Today, Switzer Financial Group offers financial advice, home loans, accounting services, as well as provding business and financial content to the general public via switzer.com.au, switzerreport.com.au and growyourbusiness.com.au.

Peter has written eight books relating to business and money, and is a highly sought after speaker on the speaking circuit. There are those who even think he's funny! He is a family man and is now a devoted "Poppy" to two grand-daughters and a grandson. While no longer an active lifesaver (Peter joined the North Bondi Surf Club when he was 13 and later became the youngest patrol captain in the Club's history) he's often seen with his family walking in Sydney's east on his way to the surf at North Bondi.

It is not the critic who counts; not the man who points out how the strong man stumbles, or where the doer of deeds could have done them better. The credit belongs to the man who is actually in the arena, whose face is marred by dust and sweat and blood; who strives valiantly; who errs, who comes short again and again, because there is no effort without error and shortcoming; but who does actually strive to do the deeds; who knows great enthusiasms, the great devotions; who spends himself in a worthy cause; who at the best knows in the end the triumph of high achievement, and who at the worst, if he fails, at least fails while daring greatly, so that his place shall never be with those cold and timid souls who neither know victory nor defeat.

The Man in the Arena speech by US President Theodore Roosevelt, at the Sorbonne in Paris, France on 23 April 1910

INTRODUCTION

"Read this and change"

Peter Switzer

If you're reading this book, you've made a great start to changing your money life forever. This book will do that. All you have to do is read it and make the necessary changes. I've kept it short and easy to follow so you will make those changes. I think two of my favourite quotes might help you read the book and make the necessary changes.

The first is: "If nothing changes, nothing changes!" And the second one is "Anything worth doing is worth doing for money!" My Dad passed away when he was 50 and Mum was 45. She was so ill-prepared to lose him in more ways than you could possibly imagine. Mum just never understood money and thought that Dad had an endless stream of it. Trouble was this stream was the result of Dad's hard labour as a small business owner and when he died, the money eventually dried up.

Mum worked hard raising us but just wasn't interested in knowing anything at all about money.

Dad never planned on dying so young. He thought he'd accumulate wealth in his 50s. So they led a comfortable life and gave their two children a good education but never hedged their own bets about their financial future.

Until Dad died, Mum had never written a cheque in her life. She had store credit cards that Dad paid off each month, after some arguments about over-use! That was the way a lot of relationships worked back then.

After Dad's passing, my wife (then girlfriend) used to sit down and explain to Mum how to write a cheque, how to be aware that her bank account couldn't be overdrawn (once she started to write cheques there was a time when she never stopped and the bank used to call!!) and other money matters that she had no idea about.

My wife and I were living in London when Dad died and we came home to help Mum. We worked in the business (it was a providore business and given the growth of cafes and restaurants over the years, Dad was on a winner). We sold it for a reasonable sum and this helped Mum settle herself financially for a while.

Maybe Mum's lack of understanding about money was a generational thing. But in my work in the financial space, I realise that there's still a reality gap about money for so many people. It's why this book, *Join The Rich Club*, is dedicated to people like my Mum, in the hope that they'll realise that having money gives them more choices than they realise. It's why I own a financial advice business. I want Australians to understand how they can have a comfortable financial life, which will enrich their material life and even their overall life. The US comedian, Sophie Tucker, once reflected on her life and said: "I've been poor and I've been rich. Rich is better." I agree!

A few months ago I went to see my Mum. After leading a long

life, her memory had let her down and she had to go into care. Mum was in a comfortable place with excellent people looking after her before she passed away recently. But her life after losing Dad could have been so much better if both of them had planned for their lives ahead.

In the future, many Australians will be more comfortable in their retirement because Paul Keating introduced compulsory superannuation decades ago, but you have to do more if you want a richer retirement.

Don't think looking after your money is just a boring super thing. I want to make super and other wealth building strategies as sexy as property, because if you knew when you were in your 30s, 40s and 50s that your wealth plan was so hot and going to deliver you great riches when you eventually stop working, you might actually be able to really enjoy your life all the time. Certainty about future riches can make for a better life today!

Now that's a really exciting and dare I say 'sexy' thought!

Getting your overall money life, your super and your property plays right is what this book will help you do. And you won't have to be a money genius to master it.

I'll help you stop just being a consumer without a plan to becoming an informed investor who builds riches.

My parents survived the Great Depression and brought me up to live within my means, save some for tomorrow, share and don't be greedy, work hard for the necessities in life knowing that money does not make you better or more important than anyone else.

David Suziki, Canadian academic, science broadcaster & environmental activist.

12 STEPS TO GET RICHER

1 Focus on what you want. Write down your goals.

4 Use the best money-making super, deposits & loans.

2 Set out a plan to get richer.

5 Learn from rich, successful people.

3 Find the money! Save smarter. Get more income.

6 Get comfortable with stocks.

When you have finished reading this book, use these 12 steps as your personal checklist so you can climb your stairway to financial heaven.

7 Become an expert user of debt & banks.

10 Become a super expert.

8 Become a property expert.

11 Become a tax expert.

9 Become a self-motivating expert.

12 Continually read "stuff" that will make you smarter and richer

01   I WILL MOTIVATE YOU TO GET RICH

"All things are ready if our mind be so."

William Shakespeare
Henry V.

The aim of this chapter is to get your mindset right to get rich. Before we talk about smart money things to do, I want you to be in the right head space.

What follows is some motivational advice from your money coach, which I have now become.

By the end of this chapter, my goal is to win you over but you have to want to change.

Why must you want to change?

Because like the great tennis champ Chris Evert said: "There were times when deep down inside I wanted to win so badly I could actually will it to happen."

I want you to want to get independently rich so badly that you too can will it to happen.

I need you to learn from Seinfeld's TV character George Costanza. George totally turned around his life, which he described as one where every decision he made was wrong. This led Jerry Seinfeld to suggest that: "If every instinct you have is wrong, then the opposite would have to be right."

George fought his instincts, did the opposite, won the attraction of a beautiful girl and got a job with the New York Yankees!

Yeah, I know this is TV, but even in the real world there are experts on psychology who'll tell you that visualisation of being successful, fit, thin, wealthier and even happier can actually work!

I want you to visualise yourself richer and getting even richer. I'm not saying you have to see yourself as James Packer rich but really comfortable and getting more comfortable by the year.

Great sporting coaches don't motivate teams with one war cry. They might have a unifying one, such as "one for all and all for one" but different individuals need different motivations to achieve maximum performance, their personal goals and, ultimately, the team's or coach's goal. There are lots of smaller personal goals that make the big collective goal, such as winning the competition, come true.

WHAT'S YOUR MONEY GOAL?

I'm arguing that the starting point for success is to have a goal, which leads to a collection of related goals. In my financial planning business, we start by asking our future clients what their goals are. We get answers like: having a million dollars when

I retire; paying off my house; being able to help my kids and grandkids to be comfortable. Few say, "I want to be rich beyond my wildest dreams" but it's OK to have a goal like that, especially if you use that money to help others.

I use 'rich' to mean being so well off that you're able to easily meet your life goals. It implies you're in an above average position, wealth-wise.

DARE TO DREAM

Some people have limited goals because they haven't dared to conceive them or they just haven't thought about it. It might be too scary. They might think they can't do much about it so they'll simply work hard, save, buy a house and see what happens. They'd do better with a financial plan that's structured to make those undefined goals come true. That's what we do with our financial planning clients and that's what I want for you.

You could learn to do it yourself, i.e. create your financial plan and this book will help with that. Or you might decide you need help. If that's a big job for you to do, then you might need to find a trustworthy adviser.

Good accountants, who get involved in a client's business, become a part of the support team that helps create great businesses and business owners/leaders. This book wants to become a part of your money life as a guiding light to building wealth and making dreams come true.

TIME TO GET IT RIGHT AND WRITE IT DOWN

There's an old saying that "if a goal is not written down, it's not on the planet!"

I want you to clearly outline your goals: life, career, business, wealth, sporting, etc. Then I want you to write it all down. That's right. Write down the goals — using a pen, computer or smart phone — and then draw up the plan to make it happen. But before that, I have to get you motivated, first to do the above and, second, to commit to the plan's programme.

JUST DO IT!

Let's make this simple to show how basic and how right my argument is. You might look in the mirror and say: "I don't look good. I'm overweight. I look soft and I look older than I am." The next thought is critical. If it's: "Oh well, I'm gonna have to avoid mirrors!" then things have to change. But if it's this: "I better get a dietician and a personal trainer", then you're going to change things.

By the end of this chapter, I'm going to get you to write down your goals and then roughly set out a plan to make them happen. But let's work on your motivation first because successful people, who turn their goals into plans that bring success, are highly motivated.

BEAT YOU AND THE LITTLE VOICE AND KICK GOALS

Having goals helps your motivation but you do have to add some more tricks, to help make it happen. Australia's Herb Elliott was the 1960 Olympic mile gold medalist, who was never beaten in international athletics. At a conference I was speaking at, I heard Herb explain why we don't make our goals happen — it's that damn little voice inside your head that's committed to failure.

Imagine you promise yourself that you'll get up and run every morning. For a month you do it, while the sun is shining and people start giving you compliments, such as "looking good Switz" and "way to go slim fella". But then the weather turns cold and it's raining in the mornings. And that's when the little voice makes an appearance. It's likely to start with: "It's raining outside and it's cold." Then it comes up with the clincher: "If you run and get the flu, then all your good work will be undone, so you better have this morning off." You agree and the little voice has won! If it rains for a week, you're back to the old you! Another win for the little voice and another loss for you.

You have to beat the little voice. Having goals is the way to do it. You have to be fanatically connected to your goals, talking about them daily. You need to have them on your screen saver with a motivational picture or whatever you come up with to remain engaged. I'm talking about changing who you are by a really small amount to start with, but this creates a snowball effect where you do more and more things that ensure the goals are kicked.

SIR BOB'S F-OFF LINE

A few years back, a colleague, who was struggling with her business challenges, cynically asked why business conference organisers will ask non-business types (e.g. sports stars, rock stars, former heroin addicts, paraplegics, mountain climbers, and so on) to address a group of business owners or executives?

Here's why.

Once upon a time, here in Australia, a business group had the former lead singer of the Boomtown Rats, Sir Bob Geldof, address them. These guys and girls were mortgage brokers and real estate agents and Sir Bob, who hasn't really run a business to my knowledge, gave one of the best bits of business advice I've ever heard. In fact, on reflection, it was advice that has powered me along in my business and other endeavours my whole life.

At the conference, a young journalist, who actually worked for my company at the time, asked Sir Bob what the best bit of advice he was ever given was that could help the business people at the conference. His answer was: "F-ck off!"

The answer quite shocked the young woman and she failed to understand that his reply was not an insulting reaction to her question but, in fact, was his considered answer.

Some weeks later, another journalist — who was not phased by Sir Bob's rude reply — recounted the story in a magazine article and pointed out that the old rock singer and humanitarian campaigner had argued that every time someone told him to "f-ck off", it made him determined to succeed.

We all need prompts, kicks in the pants or words of wisdom that jolt us out of our complacency if we want to succeed in our careers, grow a great business, create a nice pile of wealth or be a great role model for our kids or employees.

CHANGE YOUR STORY

An insult or a kick in the pants could be the jolt you need to change your story, as Tony Robbins, US life coach recommends. If your current life story isn't giving you happiness or feelings of satisfaction, then change the story.

This book is a story changer, so keep on reading.

Of course, tough love inspiration doesn't suit all personality types, though it has been useful to me, as someone who likes to prove wrong anyone who doles out injustice to P. Switzer!

GET OUTSIDE THE NORMAL PERSON'S SQUARE

When I'm asked to speak to business groups, I refer to Edward de Bono, who I interviewed years ago, who said the high achievers in business, the arts or sport, even politics, are people who think outside the square. They look at their rivals and make sure that they're able to out-compete them.

Over the years, I've been lucky enough to interview some of the best business builders this country has produced. Just listening to these high achievers always made me go back to my own business and simply try harder and work smarter. And trying to think outside the square, as de Bono recommends, has been very rewarding.

GETTING BEACHLEY-LIKE PASSION TO GET RICHER

In 2010, I took my TV show to the Shanghai Expo and we broadcasted out of the wonderful Australian pavilion. Upon entering, the 30,000 visitors a day were exposed to the icons of Australia. One of the more prominent was a huge photo of our world surfing champ — Layne Beachley.

The so-appropriately-named Beachley won the world championship seven times. And she did it despite a very challenging childhood, which could have seen lesser types go off the rails or at least under-achieve.

As a retired champion, she tried to inspire others with her Layne Beachley Foundation 'Aim for the Stars', which supports ambitious females around the country to achieve their goals.

Sometimes former sporting champions have a crack at business and aren't able to achieve the same success as they had in sport. But that's not to say they don't have a great story to inspire others. Their business under-achievements could be because they don't have the same passion for business that drove them to the top in their chosen sport, but it doesn't mean that their story can't inspire others in business.

And this is the critical message I've discovered over the years of talking to high achievers in business and sport, and after reflecting on my own successes and failures.

You must have the passion for what you're doing to get outside your comfort zone to rack up results that make you stand out from the crowd. I've learnt that just about everything in life you want is just outside your comfort zone and you have to challenge yourself to make it bigger and better.

COACH YOURSELF OR GET A COACH
The best performers in the world get the best help from experts who know more than them. They use personal trainers to look good and feel good. They use business coaches or executive coaches to get the edge in business. They employ financial advisers to invest wisely to make sure that the hard work in business results in peace of mind with their wealth in the future.

IMPORTANT

Buying this book means you're looking for inside information from an expert to get better. So congratulations!

These winners have the best accountants to minimise their tax legally and they have the best lawyers to ensure they get good advice when it is critically important.

These people have the guts to spend money on getting an edge but they're diligent with their cash flow management.

Most of all, they have the desire to win. That's the value of inspirational people — they can make you dream of success and can sometimes actually change people forever.

BETTER YOURSELF
When I was young and easily influenced by the clichés that many of us live our lives by, I was content to avoid the brutal truth. On important matters where I appeared weak, I'd dismiss them as being activities I was simply not born with the ability to do much about.

I was wrong when it came to many crucial areas, which can make a big difference to your successes and failures. Fortunately, this condition that might have held me back didn't last for a long time. I no longer believe you have to be a natural born leader to lead. You don't have to come from money to end up wealthy. You don't have to be left a business from a wealthy family to build a massive business. However, you do have to be open to luck and be flexible towards change.

On the other hand, I don't simply believe passion and hard work will always deliver business and wealth accumulation success.

All these reflections and some of my newer views on the building blocks for high achievement came back to me after reading Malcolm Gladwell's book *Outliers*. Richard Branson's *Losing My Virginity* had a similarly positive impact on me.

I'm telling you that you need to seek and read the books of these high achievers if you want to go to the next level. Jim Collins, author of *Good to Great*, says the business success stories he looked at always had a big, hairy audacious goal or a BHAG.

Gladwell's goal was to deconstruct highly successful people and work out why it happened. One of his early conclusions is that when it comes to many sports — not all but many — when you are born is really important.

He researched Canadian ice hockey teams and champions and many of them were born in the early part of the year. Why should that be so important?

Remember he worked backwards after seeing so many champs with early-year birthdays and his reasoning made a bit of sense.

First, kids born in say January who start school with kids born in November have nearly a year's growth, strength and learning on their later-born class or team mates.

They then can end up in better sports teams or classes, which means they could get better teachers, sports training and role models. The opportunities some people get over others can't be played down in understanding many high flyers' success.

Microsoft's Bill Gates was academically smart but also came from a very rich and well-connected Seattle family. A lot of this was important to his success story.

Branson was dyslexic and poor at schoolwork but he had a well-off family. However, their great asset was their support and very positive attitude towards their son.

Our own Aussie Home Loans founder, John Symond, had no family money to rely on to build his business dreams but he had a supportive family, who made him work in their many fruit shops, after school and on weekends.

I've interviewed John over the years and he says it was hard work compared to what most other kids did that made the difference, but he thanks his parents for their work ethic and the strong lessons they taught him.

Gladwell argues that having a supportive and educating family can be the critical reason why some kids do well and others don't in school, in business and in life. But that's water under the bridge. The more important question is: "If you were born late in the year, did not have parents who gave you schooling as well as business success encouragement and have not been given a competitive advantage leg up, anywhere, what are you going to do about it?"

I know the answer as I encounter people who are disappointed with their lack of success. However, when I ask: "What have you done to change your results?" the answer is often "precious little".

I know people in business who need a business coach but are too stingy to invest in success. I know company executives who need to study at a higher level but refuse to lose money this year to study and work part-time, because they're shortsighted. They're ignoring the future money that comes from investing in success.

I bumped into a friend, who was struggling with his business and his investments. I put him in touch with a great accountant and now his money life could not be better.

In fact, he says he wants to sue his old accountant for the deductions he ignored in the past and for the lack of good advice, which all had bottom line implications.

Now, my mate wasn't given the right business support when he was young but the person he should sue is himself! He knew something was wrong and did nothing until I made him act.

HERE'S HOW YOU BECOME A WINNER/OUTLIER

 If you want to be an outlier, get off your bum, be realistic and get help where you're weak.

That's the truth.

My question to you (inspired by Colonel Nathan Jessup of the film *A Few Good Men*) is: "Can you handle the truth?"

My advice gets down to:

1. Know yourself.
2. Do a SWOT on yourself — strengths, weaknesses, opportunities and threats. Play to your strengths and make your weaknesses irrelevant by changing you or getting expert help. On page 17 there's a space to write down your goals and do a SWOT on you. Make sure you fill these in.
3. Seek inspirational people to help you face the truth about yourself and make the changes necessary to succeed.
4. Employ experts to lift your performance.
5. Make the necessary changes needed for success a life commitment. And as Winston Churchill advised: "Never, never, never give up!"

10 STEPS TO KICK YOUR GOALS

A long time ago, I emceed an event featuring the US business and motivational speaker, Brian Tracy, who was fanatical about the value of goals. What follows is what I got from his talk and his book, simply called, you guessed it, *Goals.*

Your new goal to make your big goal happen might be:

Step 1: Use your strengths.

Look at what you've achieved so far and see them as stepping stones to future success. Focus on what you have got right, not wrong, and use these wins as fuel to inspire you to greater heights. Tracy calls it "unlocking your potential" and that's what this book is all about. I know you can achieve your goals but I have to convince you. So you need to do this SWOT analysis on yourself. This is an important first step goal for you. You must write down your strengths, weaknesses, opportunities and threats.

This exercise will help you determine what a sensible big goal is, how you can tap into your strengths to make it happen, the weaknesses you must make irrelevant in your life, what opportunities exist and what might stop it all from becoming a reality. Threats like your inner negative voice might be KO'd by deciding to get a personal trainer, who picks you up every morning to make sure you get out of bed!

Step 2: Take control of your life.

Stop blaming others, even if they had a role in your problems. Time spent worrying about the past stops you making the best of the future. Worrying could be a weakness and threat to success, so identify these obstacles and set a goal to get rid of them. Don't think you have to do it all by yourself.

Great business leaders like Richard Branson didn't do his

own accounting as the business grew but he had a big say in the marketing. He used, and still uses, experts to help make weaknesses go away.

Step 3: What do you really care about?

Get to know yourself better. Write it down and make sure your goals are aligned with what you care about. You might want to give your family a beautiful home with a swimming pool because you want to see your kids having fun at home. Know yourself, set your goals on page 17 and make them happen.

Step 4: Do you believe in yourself?

Be realistic about yourself as a means to help with your goal setting and making them happen. If you don't believe in free enterprise, then going into business for yourself might not make a whole pile of sense, but you could be the world's greatest public servant, academic, schoolteacher or actor! Muhammad Ali once explained his meteoric rise to become arguably the greatest boxer ever this way: "It is the repetition of affirmations that leads to self-belief and when that belief becomes a deep conviction, things begin to happen." Ali always told us: "I am the greatest" and he certainly became exactly that.

Step 5: Who are you?

When you understand more about who you really are, you then can start working on what you're here for — your purpose! Everything I've done business-wise is around my chief skill — communication. I've been a teacher, an academic, a commentator, radio/TV presenter, financial adviser and business builder. I own a communications business and financial planning operation and recently my company listed an exchange traded fund on the stock market. In all areas, I'm teaching, communicating and helping people understand what's going on. In more recent years, I've been showing people how to make money out of the information I share. I'm doing that now with you. A great goal, therefore, is to promise yourself that you'll operate in your strength zone, as a starting point to success.

Step 6: Get out of your comfort zone.

If you don't like the hard numbers that define your money life, then it's time to get uncomfortable and do things differently.

The great US President Teddy Roosevelt summed it up neatly: "Nothing in the world is worth having or worth doing unless it means effort, pain, difficulty… I have never in my life envied a human being who led an easy life. I have envied a great many people who led difficult lives and led them well." Nearly everything we want is just outside our comfort zone, so I advise you to take on and change the parts of you that hold you back.

Step 7: Hang out with successful, positive people.

If the crowd you hang around with is full of negative types, then get a new crowd! If they're your family, get some help to assist them change their attitude. It's funny but you might be setting a bad, negative, confidence-lacking lead, so changing you via hanging out with better people could be a real game and life changer.

> *"It is the repetition of affirmations that leads to self-belief and when that belief becomes a deep conviction, things begin to happen."*
>
> Muhammad Ali

Step 8: Measure your success.

Once you have set your goals and the associated plan, set another goal to measure or assess how you're going with it all. If your goal is weight loss, then a tape measure around the belly makes sense. If it's building wealth, it could be checking the value of your share portfolio or bank balance regularly. Like a business, you need key performance indicators to see how you're doing, which will tell you what you need to do to make sure your goals are achieved.

Step 9: Read about successful people.

If I wanted to be a poet, I'd read poetry and I'd read the best. If I wanted to be an entrepreneur, I'd read Richard Branson's *Losing My Virginity* and any book on Steve Jobs and Bill Gates. If I wanted to be a top share market investor, it would be books about Warren Buffett, Sir John Templeton, Ray Dalio and people of their ilk. Take notes and use them to change yourself.

Step 10: Visualise your goals and get in the zone.

When my wife and I were growing our business, we were inspired by Muhammad Ali's quote that I mentioned in step 4. We also read Napoleon Hill's *Think and Grow Rich* on Friday nights when we were having a relaxing drink. It linked up a good time with our goal to grow our business. We ended up visualising our business in five years' time. We guessed how valuable it would become and it was what we thought was a "big, hairy audacious goal", as Jim Collins, the author of *Good to Great* would advise. These actions put us in the zone and gave us something that we could regularly measure our progress against. It made us write down not only what we saw in our vision/goal but how we would make it a reality. So we took on a business partner, got access to capital and expertise, his network and even his friendship.

He helped us give our sons, who worked in the business, new leadership ideas and business knowledge. The business hit its target way before the five years was up and a public company wanted to buy half of our business!

And as I've said, we now have a listed fund on the stock market and a part of our business has been bought by another public company. Those Friday nights took us out of our comfort zone — instead of partying we were working, albeit with a glass or two of champers. But as Robert Frost once said in a poem: "Two roads diverged in a wood, and I took the one less traveled by, and that has made all the difference." Yes, a lot of it came from a really enjoyable Friday night, champagne, a change of attitude, a big commitment to setting goals and some help from Muhammad Ali! I hope this book becomes a Friday night companion as you chart a new course for your money life.

"After a colourful life that included farming, piloting steamboats, and selling insurance, Harlan David Sanders founded Kentucky Fried Chicken at the age of 65, immortalizing his 11 herbs and spices and becoming a multi-millionaire in the process. Ray Kroc did the same, beginning his legendary transformation of McDonald's into a global colossus while he was in his 50s. The truth is that it's only "too late" when you're dead. Any time before that, the dice are still in play, the dealer still has cards to deal, you still have time. It's not over till it's over."

From my friend Matthew Michalewicz's book *Life in Half a Second*

WRITE DOWN YOUR GOALS HERE

1.
2.
3.
4.
5.
6.

DO A "SWOT" ON YOURSELF

My strengths: My weaknesses:

Opportunities: Threats:

INSPIRATIONAL MAN ON FIRE
JOHN O'LEARY

"The best is yet to come"

I want to give you some advice that I received from an exceptional man at a business conference I emceed a few years ago in the US. His name is John O'Leary and he regularly emails me with inspirational takes on life and always ends his email message with the words: "The best is yet to come."

Let me sum up John O'Leary's life to try and win you over to my point of view.

When I met him, John looked like he'd been through a butcher's mincemeat machine yet he absolutely sparkled with self-belief and exuded a willingness to help everyone who entered his space. As a nine-year-old, a garage experiment went terribly wrong and his family not only lost their house, but their wonderful little boy, who was filled with so much promise, was burnt to a crisp!

After 18 weeks in hospital, losing his fingers to amputation and being covered from head to toes in bandages, as well as being tied down to a hospital bed and unable to walk, he admitted that he didn't really feel like he could do anything with his life.

Enter his physician, Dr Vitale, who had a better vision for young John. This is what he said to his young patient, who has never forgotten: "John, you may not be able to be a court reporter, but you can be a lawyer or a judge. You may not be able to play baseball again, but you can be a manager or own the team. You may not be able to be a carpenter, but you can be a general contractor and build incredible things. John, if you want to get married and raise kids and have an incredible life, you can! You are a remarkable little boy, you can still live an amazing life, and the best is yet to come for you."

You don't have to be Steven Spielberg to work out that this is an inspirational story worthy of a Hollywood blockbuster but, more importantly, it underlines two important things.

First, we all need to seek out inspirational experts in our lives, be it your accountant, your financial planner, your life coach, your business mentor, your personal trainer or whoever you need to be the best you can. It might even be a parent.

Second, you have to be open to the advice and the insights they can share with you. It means you have to be able to beat the negativity that holds so many of us back and be open to the possibilities that are always there if you are positively-inclined to see them.

John O'Leary was a lucky young man to have had a Dr Vitale in his life, but it is a powerful message to all of us – that you need to put yourself in the best of company, even if it costs you money to do so.

Too many people dismiss the power of positive thinking, but John O'Leary is not just an internationally sought-after inspirational speaker, he is married, has kids and is living the dream that most of us would love to live.

And where did it come from? That's easy — he believed Dr Vitale's advice that "the best is yet to come for you."

Build a positive approach to life and a collection of good influences and good things will come.

Let me and this book be your Dr. Vitale.

02 GET MONEY BASICS RIGHT

"You have to get your money life on the lawn, find out where you're going wrong and take action to change things."

Peter Switzer

This book gives you processes to boost your income and make you richer. Investing in the stock market, learning about investing strategies, getting the best super fund, playing property like a pro and looking for the experts to give you a money-making edge have all been drivers for this book. However, you have to put your money life on the lawn and GST your life to find money to use for investing, there are some basic steps you should sign off on to ensure you're not letting yourself down and being a burden to others. These steps include:

1. Look at your current bank accounts.
2. Check out your super fund.
3. Investigate your insurances.
4. Decide if you need health insurance.
5. Look at your credit cards.

1. GET THE RIGHT BANK ACCOUNTS

The following bank accounts are largely regarded as best-in-breed and should be used to compare other accounts before you decide where to 'bank' your money. This will keep more money in your wallet.

Take these 3 accounts and go to sites such as www.ratecity.com.au, www.finder.com.au etc. to make sure you're getting the best deal.

1. ING Orange Everyday Debit Card with zero fees.
2. The high interest savings account ING Savings Maximiser.
3. UBank USaver.

2. SUPER FUND

The Hostplus Indexed Balanced Fund charges investment costs of 0.05% or 5 cents per $100. While there is also an administration fee of $1.50 a week, or $7.50 a week for retirement income (pension) account members, the investment charge is super cheap. I'd use this to compare and contrast other funds.

WARNING

 If a cheap fund is 1% cheaper but has underperformed better funds by 2% over a long time, then it could be false economy to select your fund on costs alone. This SuperRatings table on the next page shows Hostplus has been a good long-term performer.

"The name of the game? Moving the money from the client's pocket to your pocket."

Matthew McConaughey to Leonardo di Caprio in
The Wolf of Wall Street

TOP 10 RETURNS FOR BALANCED OPTIONS*
FOR 10 YEARS TO 30 APRIL 2019 (%)

	Superfund & investment option	10 years (% each year)
1	AustralianSuper - Balanced	9.5%
2	UniSuper Accum (1) - Balanced	9.4%
3	QSuper - Balanced	9.3%
3	TelstraSuper Corp Plus -Balanced	9.3%
3	Hostplus - Balanced	9.3%
3	CareSuper - Balanced	9.3%
7	Cbus - Growth (Cbus MySuper)	9.2%
7	Mercy Super - MySuper Balanced	9.2%
7	VicSuper FutureSaver-Growth (MySuper) option	9.2%
10	Sunsuper for Life - Balanced	9.1%

Source: SuperRatings

*Returns are net of investment fees, tax and implicit asset-based administration fees. While performance data is shown to one decimal place, rankings are based on more precise, unrounded information within the SuperRatings' database. Balanced option refers to 'Balanced' options with exposure to growth style assets of between 60% and 76%.

Past performance is no guarantee that future performances will be reproduced. However, in the absence of cast iron guarantees I do like top performers over 10-year timeframes.

3. INSURANCE

Check out what insurance your super fund offers. As you take on debt and have kids, insurance becomes more important.

Don't ignore that your super fund has insurance coverage but evaluate how good it is. Give them a call and check out the cost. You should think about life insurance, total and permanent disability insurance and income protection insurance.

Ask yourself these questions:

- What if I could never work again?
- What coverage do I have?
- Is it good enough?
- Do I need access to specific occupation cover?
- Do I need more insurance?
- How can I get the best coverage at the best price?
- What would happen to the people I care for who depend on me if I unexpectedly passed away?

These questions should make you assess your current insurance position: What would happen if something goes wrong? What compensation would happen? Am I insured for the right amount at the best price for that coverage?

HOW MUCH INSURANCE DO I NEED?

This differs person to person and family to family. The starting point is to work out what you spend weekly, monthly and yearly. Once you have a number, make sure it covers you for the period that might follow an illness, accident or death!

There are plenty of online calculators you can play around with to give you a better idea but here's one from Canstar: Budget Planning Calculator: www.canstar.com.au/calculators/budget-planner-calculator/

And if you think your super will cover you, then look at this:

"According to Lifewise, research has shown that on average those with cover through their super policy have less than half the level of cover they need." (Canstar)

You better check out what your superannuation insurance offers and then work out what you might need. Call your super fund to check this.

HOME & CONTENTS INSURANCE

If you own a property, you would be mad not to have insurance in case you lost it to fire, flood or a cyclone.

Property insurance ideally should include damage caused by fire, smoke, wind, hail, the weight of ice and snow, lightning, theft and more. Property insurance also should provide liability coverage in case someone other than the property owner or renter is injured while on the property and decides to sue.

That's the building covered. You also have to consider protection from thieves and disastrous cases of bad luck. That's where contents insurance is important.

This typically includes coverage of furniture, clothing, electrical items like televisions and laptops, money and jewellery. Contents insurance can also cover fixtures like carpets, rugs and curtains. This varies from insurer to insurer.

INSURING FOR THE RIGHT AMOUNT

This example from Canstar sums up in a nutshell why you need to be covered for the right amount.

IMPORTANT

Let's say you insure your home for $150,000, but it's really worth $250,000. A bushfire sweeps through the area and does $80,000 damage to your home. Your insurer may have the right to reduce the payout in proportion to the level of under-insurance.

In this case, there might be a payment of only $48,000. Sadly, that is nowhere near enough to repair or replace a $250,000 home.

Here are some more great tips from Canstar:

"Luckily, most insurers have insurance calculators on their websites to help you estimate what you would be up for and consequently, what value home insurance or building insurance you should be looking for. The calculators will take you through a step-by-step process starting with your postcode, as building costs vary in each state. Then they should ask you for the type and style of your house, what it is made from, finishes, size, how many bedrooms, features, to calculate how much home building insurance you need. All of this is taken into account, and then you pit your estimate up against the insurer's calculator.

"Not willing to rely upon your own or the insurers estimate you can always hire a property valuer to undertake a valuation on the property. Included in this service will be an estimate on the costs to replace the building (home).

"When it comes to contents insurance, or even personal effects insurance, doing a household inventory of everything you own in your home is one of the most important steps you can take to protect your items. An inventory can help you keep track of everything, from your electronics and appliances to your jewellery and DVD collections. This can be invaluable when deciding how much contents insurance coverage you need."

CAR INSURANCE

You have to have third party property insurance in case your cheap car KO's a Mercedes or Ferrari. That will kill your getting richer aspirations.

Don't drive a car unregistered and without third party insurance as that could not only injure other human beings, it will again kill your goals to get richer. These types of insurances are all about risk management and you can't leave home in a car without them! Comprehensive insurance insures you against smashing someone's car, which could be expensive but also covers your car's damage. The more valuable your car, the more you need to think about comprehensive insurance. This is all about risk minimisation.

IT'S TIME YOU STEPPED UP AND BECAME A BARGAIN HUNTER

All these important insurances are costly so you need to become a savvy shopper and a bargain hunter.

You should be using comparison websites, comparing the price of an insurance premium to what you get for it and then you have to drive a hard bargain.

And once you find the best deal for yourself on these sites, (I list 3 of them on page 241) check out any big brand names not on the site who you can go to and twist their arms for a better deal. For example: new customers have leverage (or putting it another way you have them over a barrel). A new customer is often with an insurance company for a long time so these companies are willing to do a deal today to get you, possibly, for life!

And while on twisting financial arms, if ever you think you have been mistreated, fight with them!

Find out what consumer remedies are available to you. Threaten them with it and often they'll see reason and make up for their bad behaviour.

Since the Royal Commission, financial institutions will be mindful of bad press, so work it for all it's worth if you think you have genuinely been mistreated.

You can always go to the Australian Financial Complaints Authority (AFCA) at www.afca.org.au.

4. HEALTH INSURANCE

I'd start with the question — do I need it?

Private health insurance policies are classified into 4 tiers: basic, bronze, silver or gold. The Government has defined the tiers and the clinical services that make up each tier. For example, if you want cover for pregnancy and child birth, then you would need to take out a gold policy.

Medicare gives Australian residents access to health care and is partly funded by taxpayers who pay a Medicare levy of 2% of their taxable income. This gives you coverage in a public hospital. However, there can be a financial kick-in-the-butt from the Government if you don't have private health insurance. They will slug you with a Medicare Levy Surcharge (MLS) if your annual income is over $90,000 as a single or $180,000 as a couple or family and you're not currently covered by a registered private health insurance policy. The definition of income is complicated and I won't bore you here with it but if you have negatively geared assets and other exotic aspects to your income, check out the income definition here: www.ato.gov.au/individuals/medicare-levy/medicare-levy-surcharge/income-thresholds-and-rates-for-the-medicare-levy-surcharge/

WARNING

For a single, the medicare levy surcharge is up to 1.5% and cuts in at $90,001. At $140,001 you'll be paying an extra $2,100 in tax.

If you have an appropriate level of private patient hospital cover, you won't have to pay the MLS. And depending on your income, you may be eligible for the private health insurance rebate.

All this says that there is a Government-incentive to find a better private health insurance option to paying the MLS.

5. CREDIT CARDS PLAYED SAFELY

This is what ASIC's MONEYSMART website advises to save money on the so-called fantastic plastic:

- Try to pay off the balance within the interest-free period to avoid paying interest. If you regularly pay off your credit card balance in full, shop around for a card with no annual fee or a low annual fee, rather than a lower interest rate.

- Even if you can't pay all you owe in full, try to pay off more than the minimum repayment to reduce the amount of interest you pay. Shop around for a low-interest credit card, if you know you usually have difficulty paying the credit card balance in full each month.

- Avoid cash advances — they have no interest-free period, charge ATM fees and often incur higher interest charges

- Limit the number of credit cards you have, especially if you can't pay them off within the interest-free period. Be aware that store cards usually charge higher interest than standard credit cards.

- Make sure your credit card limit reflects the amount of debt you can manage. If you need to lower your limit, contact your credit provider and ask them to do this.

- Read your statements carefully to check that you're charged correctly. You may be able to reverse a transaction if you didn't get the goods you paid for. Contact your credit provider immediately if you discover any transactions on your statement that you did not authorise.

For more protective inside info on credit cards go to: www.moneysmart.gov.au/tools-and-resources/publications/factsheet-credit-cards-and-store-cards

FIND THE CHEAPEST CARD

The comparison websites help you start looking for the best credit card for you. Go here as a starter www.finder.com.au/revealing-the-cheapest-credit-cards but then keep searching.

When I looked, 11.99% seemed to be the cheapest rate but the ongoing fees varied bank to bank. Going to other sites I found the Community First Visa Credit Card at 8.99% but you do need to look at the fees to make sure that the rate of interest isn't actually made dearer because of the fees.

Also the interest-free period must be checked. A longer free period might make it easier for you to pay off your balance each month. Before I delve into into the chapter on property, let me share this tip with you.

TIP: SMART MORTGAGE MANAGEMENT

I think it's crazy for someone not to consider having a mortgage offset account. An offset account is a savings account linked to your home loan so that it reduces the amount of interest you have to pay. Here's an example from www.yourmortgage.com.au to simply explain how this nifty account works: "For example, let's look at Jessica's situation. Jessica has a home loan of $323,500 with an interest rate of 6.95%, and an offset account with $45,000 in it.

She earns interest on her savings at 6.95%, which equates to $260 per month. This amount is used to "offset" the interest that accrues on her loan ($1,875 per month). Consequently, her monthly interest repayment on her mortgage is reduced to just $1,615."

Other benefits include:
- Jessica pays off her loan quicker.
- She saves a load of interest.

- She reduces her tax bill as she doesn't earn interest and pocket it, therefore having to declare it in her annual income tax return, as she would in a normal savings account.

On the other hand, the fees can be hefty. You need to compare what interest rate you can get with the mortgage offset account. Clearly, the more money you have in the account, the better and bigger the saving.

Once again you need to do your homework before deciding how you will move.

INVESTING TO GET RICH

This whole book helps you to invest to get rich.

Your goals have to be to change your spending to boost your saving and/or to earn more to boost your saving. And then you have to participate in investment opportunities that have a high probability of delivering you higher returns than safe term deposits at a bank.

For the average person, this process of saving more to fund your investments should mean that they:

1. Save to buy a house and pay it off quickly. (See chapter 9.)
2. Add more to super via salary sacrifice. (See chapter 10.)
3. Aspire to buy an investment property when everyone wants to sell, with help from the Tax Office. (See chapter 9.)
4. Buy quality dividend-paying stocks when everyone wants to sell. (See chapter 7.)
5. Think of themselves as investors who have learnt from arguably the world's greatest investor, Warren Buffet of Berkshire Hathaway, when he told us: "Be fearful when others are greedy. Be greedy when others are fearful." (Read the whole book!)

HOW RICH ARE AUSSIES?

In 2013, a Credit Suisse report told us that we Aussies are the richest people in the world. Based on the median wealth of adult Australians, we stood at $US219,505 ($233,504) — the highest level in the world (Credit Suisse *2013 Global Wealth Report*).

In 2018, another report said Australia was the second-wealthiest nation in terms of wealth per adult after Switzerland. In simple terms, we are wealthy. But a 2015 OECD (Organisation for Economic Coorperation and Development) study said our high cost of living means one in three retirees live in poverty! According to an HSBC study, most Aussies run out of money 13 years before they die!

"If past history was all that is needed to play the game of money, the richest people would be librarians."

Warren Buffett

HOW DID OUR RETIREES END UP SO POOR?

Some of it was bad planning and some of it was bad luck. Here are the reasons why one in three retirees are close to the poverty line and others run out of dough before passing away:

- There was no compulsory super until Paul Keating thankfully imposed it on us.
- Once people thought a pension would get you through life but times were cheaper and personal expectations were lower.
- We're living longer than we expected and this chart proves it:

"Life can only be understood backwards; but it must be lived forward."

Soren Kierkegaard

LIFE EXPECTANCY (YEARS) AT BIRTH BY SEX, 1881–1890 TO 2014–2016

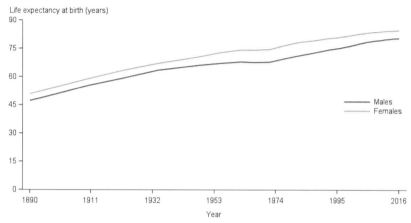

Life expectancy at birth (years)

Year

Source: Australian Institute of Health and Welfare.

Even in the 1950s, you expected to cark it in your 60s!

- Finally, people back then didn't have people like me, Ross Greenwood or Paul Clitheroe harassing them in the media to get their 'getting richer' act together!

Remember this: No one plans to fail when it comes to money and building riches. They simply fail to plan!

DON'T HAVE DEJA VU: TEACH YOUR CHILDREN WELL!

I've told you the story of my Mum and Dad. Lots of people tell me that their mum and dad were lovely people but were hopeless with money or were very careful with their savings and as a consequence never really built their wealth. Some were saved by buying a great house and holding on to it but they often were asset rich but cash poor. And many of these wonderful people lived like that so they could leave their family a valuable asset in the form of the family home.

Your job is to learn about money and to build income so you can be a great role model and a giver of wealth wisdom for your future generations. And the payoff should be that you not only teach your children well but you have a damn good time along the way!

THE MILLION DOLLAR NEST EGG GOAL

A 'million dollars in retirement' is often talked about as a goal for retirees nowadays. Those in their 50s and a long way from this nest egg often have valuable homes so they could sell up and trade back to a smaller property. If that's not an option, then there are other options.

The Association of Superannuation Funds (ASFA) says a couple could retire on $250,000 in their super fund and still get close to $60,000 a year to live on! How?

With $250,000 in super, they get a full government pension of around $35,000. You have to withdraw 5% of your super account each year so that gives you $12,500 and if you can find some part-time work for around $12,500 between you and your beloved, then you're pocketing about $60,000 between you. (Centrelink allows someone to earn $6,500 a year called a "work bonus" without the pension being affected.)

GIVE ME A MILLION DOLLARS ANY DAY

The previous plan is a good one if you can't get your super fund to $1 million. If you can and you can average a very doable 7% return, that gives you $70,000 without having to worry about doing part-time work. If you did get extra work, say for $12,500, like our retiree example above, you'd be living on $82,500 a year, which gives you a more materially enjoyable life than someone on $60,000. And remember in those years when the stock market has a ripper rise, that $70,000 could end up being $100,000. It's in these big market years that you'll be over the moon that you have a $1 million in super!

Now you're talking. The idea of having that kind of dough when you have time to travel overseas, go to sports and cultural events around the world and help the people you love, makes the million dollar goal worth shooting for!

And that's what this book is all about!

DO YOU NEED A FINANCIAL ADVISER?

That's a question only you can answer. Most advisers charge about 1% of the investible funds and if their efforts mean you average a gain better than the best super funds around 7% over 10 years, then they have paid their way. But critics of advisers think that returns are the only way you judge a financial adviser. That's not right. You can teach yourself to play tennis and guitar but with a coach or tutor you're more likely to end up a better player.

I once had to 'fight' a client who wanted to go to cash after the GFC. If he didn't have me to argue the toss, he would have missed out on the 36% bounce back of the stock market in 2009, one year after the GFC crash.

Some clients need tax advice, insights on government regulations and super rules.

I was staggered how many people were superannuation clueless in 2013, when I hosted *The Super Show* on radio station 2GB. Many 55 years or over listeners were unaware that if they opted to go on a Transition to Retirement Pension that they would pay 0% tax on their earnings in their super fund!

It was a matter of ticking a box. If they had a million dollars in superannuation and earnt 10%, that would be a saving of

$15,000 a year!

That's a big saving for not knowing the rules.

Sure, I know some financial advisers are scoundrels but there are accountants, lawyers, retailers, tradies and other service providers who don't play fair as well.

I know busy small business people who kept their super in term deposits earning 3% a year since the GFC but if they'd gone into a simple Exchange Traded Fund, they would have made about 120% since 2009!

The price of not getting advice can be a lot higher than paying advisers' bills!

Be clear on this: I'm not saying you have to have advice but it's up to you to know who you are and whether you need help to build your riches.

Like a lot of things in life, learning about money is like a puzzle. Put the pieces together bit by bit and you will find satisfaction working through the puzzle until you see a solution. The reality is that few of us are born rich. But we can do something about that if we put our minds to it.

"There is nothing more important than understanding how reality works and how to deal with it. The state of mind you bring to this process makes all the difference. I have found it helpful to think of my life as if it were a game in which each problem I face is a puzzle I need to solve. By solving the puzzle, I get a gem in the form of a principle that helps me avoid the same sort of problem in the future. Collecting these gems continually improves my decision making, so I am able to ascend to higher and higher levels of play in which the game gets harder and the stakes become ever greater."

From Ray Dalio's excellent book *Principles*.

"It is not because things are difficult that we do not dare. It is because we do not dare that they are difficult."

Seneca, Roman philosopher and statesman

03 SAVING TO GET RICH

"What's worth doing is worth doing for money."

Joseph Donohue
in Paul Dickson's *The Official Rules.*

At the risk of being called dull and boring, again let me remind you that the main game has to be to find money, save it and then invest it into income earning assets. Many money-challenged people get money and put it into the wrong things that don't generate income.

At the same time, you have to have a serious look at the disastrous debt situation you might be in. Then you have to do something about that.

There's good debt and bad debt and I'll get to that later in chapter 8 but be assured that the rich do use debt to get richer.

First up, let's understand the nature of debt. Read on...

Q. How do we wind up in debt?

A. That's easy — we want things our current income and savings can't bankroll. Houses, cars, furniture, clothing and holidays are the key culprits but some ambitious types take on debt to start a business or buy shares.

In the end, there's good debt and bad debt. Borrowing money to buy an asset that appreciates (goes up in value) or generates income is good debt. Cars are famous for depreciating the minute you drive them out of the car yard. A car is a classic creator of bad debt (apologies to car salespeople!) unless you use it to be an Uber driver or do deliveries for income!

Q. OK, I get bad debt (borrowing for fun things!) but what is good debt?

A. A lot of experts tell you tax-deductible debt is generally good debt but it has to also bring capital gain. This means, for example, if you buy an investment property for $800,000 and in three-years' time you sell it for $1 million — the capital value of your property has gone up by $200,000 (or 25%). Borrowing for shares, a business or income-generating activity is good debt because it's tax deductible. (Of course, if the business fails, it would be a bad outcome but the borrowings would still be tax deductible, so at least you'd share your pain with the Tax Office!) However, I'd argue that buying a home to live in for $800,000 and selling it for $1.6 million in 10 years' time with no capital gains tax is also good debt. Be aware that there is no capital gains tax on a home you have lived in as your principal property and you have not rented it out anytime for money. By the way, you could rent it out for six years because you were forced to live overseas or interstate for work purposes and there'd be no capital gains tax, provided you moved back in before the seventh year started.

If you were going to do this, check with your accountant. If you chose to rent out your principal property to make money and you did it for three years out of the 10 years you owned it, then you'd pay capital gains tax on 3/10s of the gain in the value of the property over that time. Of course, you'd only pay the tax when you sell the property. Best to run this past an accountant too.

Note in these good debt cases, it's implied that saving has been done to help you make the payments and then tax deductibility has helped the saving effort. That's why I now want to concentrate on how you can save better.

Q. How can we become less prone to bad debt?

A. If you're living a life that always ends up with a constantly rising, debt-ridden bottom line, try doing the opposite. (In other words, as I said on page 2 take a leaf out of George Costanza's book!) For the uninitiated, it's called saving.

Q. How do you become a saver?

A. There are lots of boring recommendations — like stop spending and you will instantly see savings. However, the best starting point is to do a budget. I know you might not want to do this but if nothing changes, nothing changes!

Come clean, bite the bullet, do a budget.

Q. How do you do a budget?

A. Pick up a pen and fill in the blanks on the monthly budget over the page. Come on, do it now — "if it's going to be, it's up to me!" I mean you, not me!

MY MONTHLY BUDGET

ITEMS	$ SPENT PER MONTH
Holidays (these are important!)	
Mortgage/rent	
Other loan repayments	
Credit cards approx amount	
Food	
Petrol	
Alcohol	
Cigarettes (Quit!)	
Public transport/taxi/Uber	
Books (like this one!)	
Newspapers, etc.	
Entertainment: movies etc.	
Sports events/gym membership	
Hairdressers, grooming	
Gifts (Christmas, Easter etc.)	
Childcare	
Clothing	
Eating out	
Allowances to kids	
Council rates	
Water rates	

Car rego	
Car insurance	
Car repairs	
School fees	
Health insurance	
Telephone/mobile	
Donations	
Subscriptions e.g. Netflix	
Daily Coffee x 30	
Electricity/ gas	
Pharmacy	
Doctor fees	
Dentist fees	
Pets	
Other	
MONTHLY EXPENSE TOTAL (a)	

Now for the scary bit...

Put your monthly income here $ ....(b)

Put your monthly expense total here $ ....(a)

Deduct the bottom from the top (b - a) $ _____ (c)
b - a = c (your savings!)

If you're game, take this monthly saving amount (c) and multiply it by 12 to see your annual saving or dis-saving.

....(c) x 12 months = ...
(A big ✓ if this is positive)

What it means and what you have to do…

This exercise can be nearly as scary as standing on a set of scales after an overseas trip or after Christmas Day lunch. If it's a big positive, you're sitting pretty in stage one of the "how to get rich" stakes. If it's a small positive, well, that's a start. But if it's a negative, then you have a lot of work to do.

Remember, stage one is to find the money. Stage two is to do smart things with it.

TIME TO GST YOUR LIFE!

OK, you might say "I see where my money is going, what now?" It's time to GST your life!

That's right, you need to tax yourself 10%. If you spend $50,000 a year and you can cut your spending by 10%, then you have $5,000 a year in savings. I can then show you how to invest this amount to get richer.

8 WAYS TO SAVE 10% OF YOUR INCOME

For starters try these ideas:

1. Switch home loans — for example, Switzer Home Loans are 3.59% a year at the time of writing. Use this as a benchmark and compare it against your loan and lower your monthly repayments. If you can do better, then well done you!
2. Switch credit cards — the best credit card I found on the

comparison websites such as ratecity.com.au is 8.9% with small fees. Use this for comparison.

3. Shop in cheaper suburbs.
4. Shop at discount stores or online. Even try Op shops!
5. Go to iSelect and similar websites to get the best deals out there for energy, phone, health insurance etc.
6. Drink less expensive alcohol.
7. Look at every line of expense and ask: "How can I lower this amount?"
8. Bring your lunch to work!

TIP

Aim to cut by 10%, but if you can do better — what you save in one area might make up where you can't cut, say for example with your rent. That said, if you want to be rich tomorrow, you might have to slum it today by moving to a cheaper suburb or even move home with Mum and Dad! Let's hope my kids don't read this bit of advice!

LET'S BE FAIR

If your bottom line is embarrassingly bad but you have superannuation, then your future position is partly looked after. But note, I said only 'partly' looked after.

Q. What do you mean?

A. Well, many people think they have superannuation, which means they should retire safely. That's an unsafe assumption.

Q. How come?

A. The following super facts can be scary. If you have a weak heart, close the book now and return your head to your old hole in the sand! The Association of Superannuation Funds of Australia (ASFA) suggests that for a reasonable retirement life, on average, we would want about 60% of our pre-retirement income. So, if you were on $1,000 a week before leaving work, $600 a week would save you from staying at home and watching reruns of Judge Judy on television every day and thinking you were having a really good time. By the way, in 1996 my sister Kaye created the Judge Judy programme and doesn't Judy have her to thank for turning a modestly paid but outspoken New York District Court Judge into the world's highest paid TV host in 2018, with a net worth of over $400 million (according to *Forbes Magazine*).

Q. How much must I have in super if I want to get a 60% figure in retirement?

A. For the average person, ASFA says you need to sock away, now wait for it, 15% of their income for, wait for it again, 40 years!

Q. But what if I have only 20 years of work left?

A. You'll have to put away a whole lot more.

Q. Couldn't I just take the pension?

A. You could, but under my reckoning, the pension is the biggest incentive to get into a saving strategy. Right now, the maxium basic pension rate for a single person comes in at the princely — or is it pauperly? — sum of $926.20 a fortnight. That said, if a couple has about $250,000 in super and own their home, then the full pension plus super can give you an OK life. But you won't be rich. A couple could get $36,000 on the full pension, While a single person could get $24,000.

Q. What do super funds return on average?

A. Around 6-8% per annum (before inflation) is a safe figure but they can be better and they can be worse.

Q. Don't super funds guarantee returns?

A. No, they just make what they might call 'safe projections', but they can be wrong.

Q. How do I find the best super funds?

A. Look on the next page as I've collected the best 3-year performers to 2019 and many of these have consistently been great performers. Compare your fund against these on performance and cost. If yours doesn't measure up, dump them.

WARNING

Make sure you compare apples with apples. If you have ticked the box on a conservative investment option for your super fund, you can't compare it to a balanced or growth option. In the following chart I look at the best balanced option funds, which most people are in. Have a look at returns of some well-known super funds but before you do, let me take you through some defintions:

1. Conservative option: this is a low risk option with little or no exposure to the stock market. It offers safe but low returns.

2. Growth option: this is a higher risk, very exposed to the stock market.

3. Balanced option this might be 60-70% exposed to the stock market.

Chapter 10 goes into detail on superannuation but I'm talking about it here because adding to your super can be a great way to do "forced" savings.

TOP 10 RETURNS FOR BALANCED OPTIONS*
FOR 3 YEARS TO 30 APRIL 2019

	Superfund & investment option	Return over a 3 year period
1	Hostplus - Balanced	10.9%
2	AustralianSuper - Balanced	10.3%
3	Mercy Super - MySuper Balanced	10.2%
3	Sunsuper for Life - Balanced	10.2%
5	First State Super - Growth	9.9%
5	Club Plus Super - MySuper	9.9%
7	UniSuper Accum (1) - Balanced	9.8%
8	Media Super - Balanced	9.7%
8	Cbus - Growth (Cbus MySuper)	9.7%
8	Vision SS - Balanced Growth	9.7%

Source: SuperRatings

*Returns are net of investment fees, tax and implicit asset-based administration fees. While performance data is shown to one decimal place, rankings are based on more precise, unrounded information within the SuperRatings' database. Balanced option refers to 'Balanced' options with exposure to growth style assets of between 60% and 76%. Past performance is not a reliable indicator of future performance.

BECOME A SUPER EXPERT

As I said, in Chapter 10, I'll make you a super expert. I'll show you how to get more money into super if that's the road to riches you want to travel on. For now, however, I just want to show you where the money might come from.

In Chapter 6, I will show you how $10,000 becomes $471,593 in 39 years. The more money I can help you find and the more I can show you how to invest wisely, the quicker you'll get on that road to a rich heaven. (If you can't wait go to page 76)

Q. Should my super goal as a minimum be a saving of 15% of income for 40 years?

A. You got it.

Q. The safe way would be to do it with super?

A. Yes, but if you want to be more relaxed in retirement or even "cleanly" rich (I hate the term 'filthy rich') then all the experts advise that you should be saving more than 15% in more diverse investments, giving you possibly higher returns.

DIFFERENT TYPES OF SAVING

Q. Is paying off a house saving?

A. Yes it is and if you have no qualms about selling your house in retirement and trading back later in life, then you could possibly unlock the wealth saved in your home. On the other hand, if you want to live in your home on retirement and leave it to your kids, then you need to be more enterprising. That means you have to find the money for savings and transfer it to great investments.

Q. Any other ways with property?

A. Refinancing your loan to a lower interest rate and paying more than you have to, are great ideas. Have a look at this example from what we do at Switzer Home Loans.

Assumptions:

- The average home loan in Australia is a bit over $350,000 so I've assumed that's your loan amount.

- The current rate you're paying is 5% and the refinance rate is 4%.
- The loan term is 25 years.

If you switch to the lower rate, you'll save approximately $59,500 over the life of the loan, just by paying the minimum repayments. If you get clever and retain the repayment level that you're paying on the 5% loan, you will save an additional $35,000.

By switching from a loan with a rate of 5% to a 4% product and maintaining your repayment level, you can save almost $95,000 over the term of the loan. I think this point is made pretty well. (Go to our home loan calculator to see how you can save money by either finding a lower home loan interest rate or by paying more off your loan at a faster rate. www.switzerhomeloans.com.au/advice-centre/calculators/)

> *"Rule No. 1: Never lose money. Rule No. 2: Never forget rule No. 1."*
>
> Warren Buffett, the Oracle of Omaha

BE A BUSINESS

One guy who dedicated his life to educating Australians about the link between budgets, saving and getting rich was Stuart Moore. Many years ago, he wrote a book with the smart title *How to Start With No Savings and Get Rich… Safely.*

He not only advised keeping a budget, he insisted people should keep financial records of their income and spending each week. It's like running your life like a business.

IMPORTANT

Once you track your spending, you can monitor how your budget is going. If you are not happy with your savings amount, you could set yourself a goal to cut your spending by say 10%. If you spend $500 a week and save $50, that's $2,600 for the year. Do this for nine years between the ages of 22 to 30 and plough it into the best super fund, which could return 9% per annum on average and you're looking at an easy $500,000 or more by the age of 65.

THE MORE YOU EARN

Obviously, the more you earn, the more you can save and the more you can invest and the more you can laugh as you make your way to the bank!

Q. So what's the goal?

A. Get richer and you'll do that by earning more, saving more and investing more. And do it for as long as you can. However, it is possible to save more without earning more. Once you get the saving part right, then the earning bit will also follow.

Q. This is easier said than done, isn't it?

A. Yes, but I will try to make it as painless as possible. Read on...

"It's not supposed to be easy.
Anyone who finds it easy is stupid."

Charlie Munger, American investor and philanthropist.

04 GETTING YOU IN THE RICH ZONE

"The best is yet to come"

John O'Leary

Read this if you're worried about being poor and would prefer to be rich! And read this if the four-letter word d-e-b-t worries you.

To destroy your debts or to master them to make mega-money, you have to understand the secrets of smart money management. Yeah, I'll admit that money information is not quite as interesting as watching Fox Sports or *House of Cards* but it sure has more potential to elevate your material life. After all, beneath our more sincere characteristics, most of us are material girls and boys.
It can be hard to save. It can be hard to select good investments and keep on top of money news and education. And it can also be hard coping with this expensive world with very little dough in your kick.

MONEY'S BORING — YEAH, RIGHT

Understanding money for most men and women brings a typical Homer Simpson-like mental response of "Boring". Similarly, I vaguely recall a Gary Larson cartoon where a bunch of dogs were sitting around a dining room table looking bored out of their brain. The caption went something like: "Everyone was having a great time until Sally brought up the subject of 401K funds." For Australians who don't get the joke, the term "401K funds" could be replaced with "superannuation".

On the other hand, few would debate the aged and wise view of US comedian, Sophie Tucker, who concluded:

"I have been rich and I have been poor.
Rich is better."

The plain facts are not debatable. Firstly, we should all want to know about money — specifically, how to get lots of it. At the same time, however, we don't want to suffer the fate of actually learning about it.

What lies before you is one man's struggle to make money matters actually worth reading and understanding. And while there are piles of financial facts we all should be moneywise about, the end goals in this little book are simple — how can someone destroy debt? And on the other hand, if you're not scared of borrowing, how can you use debt to get rich?

PUT YOUR HOUSE ON THIS TAX TIP

I've always argued that owning your own home and eliminating the debt against it as quickly as possible is a key wealth-creation strategy. Yes, that's right, knocking off debt not only saves you years of interest but these savings can be re-routed into some other dollar-earning investment — a rental property, more superannuation, an investment fund, etc. Go to www.switzerhomeloans/advice-centre/calculators and click extra repayments and see what can be saved by even small extra payments.

And it's very tax-effective because when you sell your principal property (the one you live in) you don't pay capital gains tax.

Some people like the *Rich Dad Poor Dad* option, borrowing money to buy rental properties because they like the tax deductions. I'll show you later how that works. Some people avoid owning a home and instead borrow to invest in stocks or investment funds. The interest repayments on these borrowings, like an investment property, are also tax deductible.

Yep, the Tax Office will help you borrow to buy shares!

APPLES WITH APPLES?

The old warning that you're not comparing apples with apples applies when you try to line up different kinds of investments.

I'll do a principal property versus investment property comparison in Chapter 9. Anyone who took the high-flying investment option would have to pay rent the whole time because they won't have a principal property. The bricks and mortar asset that you can live in has a certain feel good appeal as well, but there are no tax savings that you can access every week to help you pay back your interest. Don't worry, I will explain that little pearl as well, soon. Stick with me on this and I'll show you some neat money-making tricks.

Another plus for property, say when you compare it to shares, is that the prices of houses tend to resist the forces of gravity better than individual share prices. But some properties can have big falls. Ask anyone who owned a home on the Gold Coast in Queensland or Palm Beach in Sydney when the GFC hit.

All these options will be looked at later in the book and clearly anyone wanting to build wealth and/or kill debt needs to know this kind of stuff.

Most people want to get rich safely. This is my main game throughout this book. However, for those hell-bent on flying in the fast lane, that will be a subject for another book.

WARNING

Don't be fixated on property as the best investment for growing wealth. It's good and can be great, but don't close your eyes to other ways.

In case you haven't noticed, I've been trying to make you think differently and outside the square. So look at this little comparison story that challenges the everyday Australian's idea about how great property is compared to say stocks.

Let's imagine you're back in early 2009 and you're left $1 million by a dearly departed relative. You decide to buy an investment property in Paddington in Sydney, which has been one of Australia's most reliable suburbs for property buyers. That house would now be worth $2.5 million, which means you have made $1.5 million on $1 million, which is a return of 150%.

But what if you were a different thinker and put your money into CBA shares. What would the return have been? In early March 2009, the share price was $27. Now it's $70 so that would be a 160% gain!

If you used your relative's inheritance or you could've borrowed $1 million in early 2009, you would have bought 37,037 shares and that would've turned into $2.59 million!

On top of the better price or capital gain, you would've received great dividends, which now would give you a yield of 16% on your original investment. And with franking credits, it's more like 22%! And all this comes with no tenants, real estate agents, repairs or maintenance.

I'm not trying to turn you off property (from which I've made a lot of good money over the years), but I am trying to turn you on to the opportunities that are there with stocks as well.

Note, both investments would attract capital gain. However if the property was for you to live in there'd be no capital gain but no tax deductible interest.

THE GAME PLAN IS SIMPLE

Try to get as much of your money as you can into income generating things instead of pouring it down the consumer spendthrift's gurgler.

WANT PROOF?

Look at the table and the stories on the next page.

After you understand the bottom line, which I'll explain to you later, you will look at spending, saving and debt from an entirely different point of view for the rest of your life. This changed attitude will push you one step closer to a wealthier future and take you one step away from the poor house.

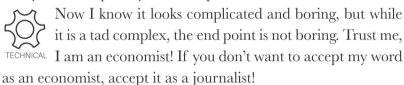 Now I know it looks complicated and boring, but while it is a tad complex, the end point is not boring. Trust me, TECHNICAL I am an economist! If you don't want to accept my word as an economist, accept it as a journalist!

Sure, it looks like a table constructed by a person who likes numbers but once again, let me insist, the final story associated with this table is memorable. Trust me. Read on...

Age	Eddy the early starter			Lucy the late starter		
	Savings per year	Total annual return 9%	Total portfolio	Savings per year	Total annual return 9%	Total portfolio
22	$2,000	$180	$2,180	$0	$0	$0
23	$2,000	$376	$4,556	$0	$0	$0
24	$2,000	$590	$7,146	$0	$0	$0
25	$2,000	$823	$9,969	$0	$0	$0
26	$2,000	$1,077	$13,047	$0	$0	$0
27	$2,000	$1,354	$16,401	$0	$0	$0
28	$2,000	$1,656	$20,057	$0	$0	$0
29	$2,000	$1,985	$24,042	$0	$0	$0
30	$2,000	$2,344	$28,386	$0	$0	$0
31	$0	$2,555	$30,941	$2,000	$180	$2,180
32	$0	$2,785	$33,725	$2,000	$376	$4,556
33	$0	$3,035	$36,761	$2,000	$590	$7,146
34	$0	$3,308	$40,069	$2,000	$823	$9,969
35	$0	$3,606	$43,675	$2,000	$1,077	$13,047
36	$0	$3,931	$47,606	$2,000	$1,354	$16,401
37	$0	$4,285	$51,890	$2,000	$1,656	$20,057
38	$0	$4,670	$56,561	$2,000	$1,985	$24,042
39	$0	$5,090	$61,651	$2,000	$2,344	$28,386
40	$0	$5,549	$67,200	$2,000	$2,735	$33,121
41	$0	$6,048	$73,248	$2,000	$3,161	$38,281
42	$0	$6,592	$79,840	$2,000	$3,625	$43,907

Steady Eddy, the early starter

The above table shows that if Eddy socks away $2,000 a year for only nine years (that is, between 22 years of age and 30) and then parties for the rest of his life until he retires at 65, then the delivered nest egg would be $579,468. This assumes an annual return of 9%, which is a fairly strong rate to use for a long-range calculation, but they were devised by an optimistic Yank!

Eddy

43	$0	$7,186	$87,025	$2,000	$4,132	$50,038
44	$0	$7,832	$94,858	$2,000	$4,683	$56,722
45	$0	$8,537	$103,395	$2,000	$5,285	$64,007
46	$0	$9,306	$112,701	$2,000	$5,941	$71,947
47	$0	$10,143	$122,844	$2,000	$6,655	$80,603
48	$0	$11,056	$133,900	$2,000	$7,434	$90,037
49	$0	$12,051	$145,950	$2,000	$8,283	$100,320
50	$0	$13,136	$159,086	$2,000	$9,209	$111,529
51	$0	$14,318	$173,404	$2,000	$10,218	$123,747
52	$0	$15,606	$189,010	$2,000	$11,317	$137,064
53	$0	$17,011	$206,021	$2,000	$12,516	$151,580
54	$0	$18,542	$224,563	$2,000	$13,822	$167,402
55	$0	$20,211	$224,774	$2,000	$15,246	$184,648
56	$0	$22,030	$266,803	$2,000	$16,798	$203,446
57	$0	$24,012	$290,815	$2,000	$18,490	$223,936
58	$0	$26,173	$316,989	$2,000	$20,334	$246,271
59	$0	$28,529	$345,518	$2,000	$22,344	$270,615
60	$0	$31,097	$376,614	$2,000	$24,535	$297,150
61	$0	$33,895	$410,510	$2,000	$26,924	$326,074
62	$0	$36,946	$447,456	$2,000	$29,527	$357,601
63	$0	$40,271	$487,727	$2,000	$32,364	$391,965
64	$0	$43,895	$531,622	$2,000	$35,457	$429,422
65	$0	$47,846	**$579,468**	$2,000	$38,828	$470,249
	$18,000			**$70,000**		

Source: The Complete Idiot's Guide to Getting Rich, Larry Waschka

Live it up Lucy, the late starter

OK, let's look at the party animal who gets serious at age 31. Lucy starts putting in $2,000 at 31 and keeps it up until 65. That means she saves for 35 years and puts in $70,000. Look at her bottom line — $470,249.

Lucy

Eddy puts in $18,000 and collects $579,468. Read on...

By getting your money knowledge and plans right, and letting compound interest cut loose, the final dividend can be sensationally rewarding.

Obviously, the intention here is to help you get your dollars heading in the right direction and make the ordeal of learning the in and outs of money more sufferable. As a compassionate person, in many of the chapters that follow, I'll try to keep as much of the 'boring' stuff wrapped up in question and answer form. And where possible, I'll be typically Switzerish — witty, bordering on banal; flippant yet relevant and pursuing the even message in the oddest way possible! That's my promise.

If I can keep you reading this book, I know I've done my job.

THE GURU'S GUIDE TO GETTING IN THE RICH ZONE

Some years ago, I wrote the Aussie version of *The Complete Idiot's Guide to Getting Rich* for US money expert Larry Waschka, who pinpointed the 7 winning habits of successful wealth builders. Here they are:

1. Save every month. (Great idea!)
2. Stay out of debt. (However, good debt can be a good wealth-builder!)
3. Shop around before buying. (Yep, it's a big saver.)
4. Don't be afraid to buy pre-loved goods. (Yep.)
5. Take care of your stuff. (So basic but so smart!)
6. Become a share market player. (Tick!)
7. Take time to plan your future. (Spot on and this book will help you do that.)

MONEY SECRETS

That's what's coming your way. If you follow these secrets, you will be richer than if you decide to ignore your money future. If you ignore your money future, like many Aussies, one day you will have hip-pocket future shock!

I don't want that for you. I simply want to make you richer. And I mean that, sincerely.

GET MORE OUT OF LIFE

I know I'll cope some flack for the title of this book and my desire to make you richer. I don't care — this type of critic doesn't count. I'm not driven by my desire to get wealthy at the expense of happiness. In fact, I've never chased wealth in my life – it has followed me. I guess I was lucky to be born with a positive attitude. I throw myself into things at both the business and personal levels. This seems to attract good people to me. When you live a life based on good values, money will follow you and good people will want to hang out with you. Get your life right first. Don't chase money. Money is a means to an end. The end goal is always happiness.

CONSIDER READING MORE

In a world where not enough people are reading the right stuff, give yourself a competitive advantage in creating a great career, a brilliant business or a wonderful family by exposing yourself and your family to the best that business has thrown up. It's a nice thought that real core values could be at the core of success.

MAUREEN'S STORY

"I learnt from my parents that money doesn't come easily"

How I came to be working for a financial services firm called Switzer Financial Group is a long story but let me simply say that "money" is part of my DNA. I come from a long line of chartered accountants and my Mum, who was gifted in numeracy, basically ran a wholesale grocery business,

that is, until she met Dad. She had to give up her job – that was the way things operated in those days. My parents met 'later' in life. Mum was atypical of her times – I think she could have been a high flyer if she never married or had kids.

My parents proceeded to have seven children in 13 years, with me being their last – the spoilt one, they often say.

Mum ran our household like a business – private schools, no credit cards, no frills. I shadowed my Mum all my young years and used to watch her doing budgets, and strictly adhering to them. There were tins and jars where money was dispatched to pay light bills, gas bills and incidentals. There wasn't a roof space or cupboard where a container with money wasn't stashed. Dad was an engineer and for many years worked at Commonwealth Engineering, where former Prime Minister Paul Keating's father also worked for a time. He was on a good wage but not one that easily stretched to educating a large family. My maternal grandparents were set to live with us but Grandpa died, so Grandma moved in and I shared a room with her.

There was always food on the table and education was priority number one. My parents went without most things to ensure that. Like one of my brothers, I won a scholarship, which helped alleviate the constant strain of making ends meet. When both sets of grandparents passed away, there was an inheritance from each side. Mum and Dad paid off their mortgage, bought a new car, put money in the bank and we had holidays. But most of the time when I was young I saw my Mum battle. She managed the money and how she did this baffles me to this day.

I learnt from my parents that money doesn't come easily. For most people, it's the result of hard work. I learnt the value of money and the importance of budgeting from my Mum and it has proved so valuable to me throughout my life. Dad would have given you the shirt off his back but Mum always had to be judicious and watch every penny.

When Peter and I started to accumulate our wealth, I used to buy Mum beautiful things that she gave up for us. Peter says in this book that having money gives you the opportunity to help others and this is true.

Mum and Dad didn't have a lot but they still helped others. My parents not only raised seven children, they cared for their own parents, fostered many children over the years and were active in the community. Some people have money and keep every penny for themselves and that's their prerogative. But being able to help others is such a good thing to do for yourself and for those you assist. Learning about money and growing your wealth makes helping others and being independent yourself totally achievable.

05 RICH SMART STUFF SMARTIES KNOW

"Success comes from knowing what you don't know more than coming from what you do know."

Ray Dalio, US investor, philanthropist

The respected business journalist, Elizabeth Knight, writing in *The Sydney Morning Herald* posed the question: "Where are the answers to our problem banks?" The answer isn't right in front of you but it's not all that far away either.

Of course, for a country so worried about our banks, where 68% of people wanted a Royal Commission (according to a poll by The Australia Institute), it might be a good idea if we stopped being experts on such trivial matters, such as why Andrew Fifita wasn't selected for the NRL's Kangaroos, Kim Kardashian and the Budgie Nine at the Malaysian Grand Prix. (If you don't remember any of these unimportant news stories, well good on you!)

Yep, if the country has a bank problem, then sure, let's get the Government acting to protect people but also let the people of the country help solve it themselves by wising up, reading smart stuff and hanging out with the right crowd.

DON'T JUST BLAME THE BANKS! BLAME YOU TOO!

How come "caveat emptor" (let the buyer beware) works in so many aspects of our retail life but somehow we need excessive protection from our banks? Yes, some bank behaviour definitely needs changing. In reality, however, we need protection from our own indifference towards getting richer and from our unprofessional ways when it comes to something really important — our money.

I'm going to list a few really sensible things that all Australians should know to bullet-proof their money life. And you don't need another big brother Government inquiry to deliver you results that will protect you from the hip-pocket threats out there.

DO THESE THINGS TO IMPROVE YOUR BOTTOM LINE

1. I've said this before and I'll say it again. Create a list of all the financial products you have —from your super fund to bank accounts to insurance policies to loans. Go through each policy, noting all costs and/ or returns from them.

2. Go to comparison websites such as www.finder.com.au, www. ratecity.com.au, www.iSelect.com.au, www.superratings.com. au, and so on to make sure you have great deals on loans, term deposits, credit cards, insurance policies, energy prices, leases, etc.

3. If you're 50 plus, join the FiftyUp Club from my mates at 2GB/3AW/4BC/6PR and the Macquarie radio network at www.fiftyupclub.com for a range of money-saving deals.

4. Go to a mortgage broker to see if you have the best home loan deal or simply see if you can do better than www. switzerhomeloans.com.au, where our variable home loan rate

is 3.59% with no fees, etc. Our advertised and comparison rates of interest are exactly the same, unlike a lot of lenders. (Sorry about the plug but I'm plugging everyone else and we do have a great, damn honest deal!)

5. Importantly, find out what your super fund costs and returns. Then compare it to this list:

TOP 10 PERFORMING GROWTH FUNDS*
FOR 15 YEARS TO SEPTEMBER 2018 (%)

Ranking	Superfund & investment option	15 years (% pa)
1	AustralianSuper Balanced	8.5%
1	Hostplus Balanced	8.5%
3	Catholic Super Balanced (MySuper)	8.4%
3	Cbus Growth (Cbus MysSuper)	8.4%
5	CareSuper Balanced	8.3%
5	UniSuper Balanced	8.3%
5	QSuper Balanced	8.3%
8	BUSSQ Balanced Growth	8.2%
8	Rest Core	8.2%
8	TelstraSuper Balanced	8.2%

Source: Chant West Pty Limited (www.chantwest.com.au).

*Disclaimer: The Chant West data is based on information provided by third parties that is believed accurate at the time of publication. Past performance is not a reliable indicator of future performance. Your objectives, financial situation and needs have not been taken into account by Chant West and you should consider the appropriateness of this information, and read the relevant Product Disclosure Statement, before making any decisions.

6. Switch your 17-20% credit card to the ME Frank Credit Card at 11.99% or the Coles Low Rate MasterCard at 12.99%.

7. Check out the ING Everyday Debit Card with zero fees. ING's savings maximizer is also a good benchmark account.

Once you have all your information together and you know what you're paying and what you could be paying, go to your bank and twist some arms for matching or better deals. This is just a 7-step plan to get you money smart and to protect your hip pocket from the scary world of banking, which we make scarier than it has to be by being so unprofessional about how we operate with money. One day you might find trustworthy accountants and financial planners who'll help you grow your wealth. And out of that, you can teach your children about what an adult should know and be doing about money.

WARNING

 If you don't do this stuff ASAP, you probably don't really care about getting richer, so you may as well blame the banks for your future relative poverty!

PARENTAL EXAMPLE HAS TO BE MONEY-POSITIVE

A few years back, 2GB's Alan Jones referred a listener to my financial advice business. This person was in hot water after borrowing too much for a home and business. He needed help but said he was encouraged to over-borrow by his dad! He reflected on his life and admitted that his old man had been a bad role model. This guy actually cried as he asked me to show him how he could be a good money example for his kids.

He potentially was going to lose his business, his house and wife, which can be powerful motivators to lift your money game. As I always joke, if anything is worth doing, it's worth doing for money. As parents, it's even bigger than just the bottom line — we need to give great guidance to the ones we love.

I hope this little education piece spurs on many to lift their game. My greatest fear is that not enough people will read this book. Spread the word about what I'm writing to friends and family. We need this money message to go viral!

 Every morning on *Switzer Daily* (www.switzer.com.au) I try to make the world of money, finance and getting richer easier to understand. Reading me (or someone else who also does this) might be a great first step to bulletproofing your money life from all the threats out there. That said, the greatest problem is our lack of commitment to building our wealth — and only you can change that.

WHAT MONEY SMARTIES KNOW

Here's a quick Q&A on what the smarties know about getting rich. Gordon Gekko, in the movie *Wall Street*, lectured us: "if you are not inside, you're out!"

Let me try and get you into the inner circle when it comes to money.

Q. What do we want?

A. To be wealthier.

Q. When do we want it?

A. Now would be ideal but if that can't be arranged, when we retire would be the worst-case alternative.

Q. What do smart guys and gals know about getting wealthy?

A. There are basic game plans and goals, which maximise the chances of wealth coming your way and minimise the likelihood of poverty.

Q. Can you show us how to build our wealth from the beginning to the end?

A. By all means.

Q. So what do I need to know?

A. In a nutshell, collect a basket of investments or assets — cash, shares, property, superannuation, investment funds, even artwork, etc. — and keep them for a good amount of time.

Q. How do I find the money for this "oh so simple" plan?

A. You need to reduce the high cost of a 'wasteful life', which means you will build up savings. Get a second job or start a part-time business to get extra money or even move back home with your parents, if they're open to that! Get thinking 'outside the square' to get the dough to grow your riches! Time and compound growth will do the rest.

Q. Compound growth, what's that?

A. When an investment rolls over and over with interest kicking in year in and year out, then compounding of the growth of the investment produces surprisingly healthy results. The Rule of 72 explains it all.

Q. What's the Rule of 72?

A. The number crunchers (call them mathematics geeks) have worked it out. It says that if someone promises you 6% interest or return on an investment, it will take 12 years for the amount invested to double. The compounding process is such that if you were given 12% a year, then you would double your dough in six years!

Q. How come?
A. 72 divided by 12 = 6 years. 72 divided by 6 = 12 years.

Q. How come?
A. Look, you don't need to know. Trust me, I am an economist.

Q. If we say that a good super fund returns around 8% a year, we should expect our money to double in nine years — is that right?
A. Yes that should be your expectation. Some funds can even do better than that. Finding out the names of these (see page 67 for the better super funds) and how often they beat 8% is something you should be interested in. (I'll rename some later, so stick with me.)

Q. Is doing better than 8% over a long time common?
A. No, many of these funds are more risky investments than conservative funds, and they promise to be exactly that, but that's why their returns can be very good. If the stock market goes belly up, the returns can nosedive. That said, the above 8% super funds are pretty safe. I wouldn't worry about my money being in those funds in the table on page 67, provided I have time on my side.

Q. But it's all very well to say, save and get a bunch of productive investments. But how do I get the 'inside' information? And are there traps?
A. For the first question, just keep reading this book. Then read others and get money smart. And yes, there are many traps.

Q. What traps?

A. Understanding risk is one, for starters. In the example above, if anyone offers you an 18% return, (which means your money doubles in four years), then the high return instantly means the risk is high. On the other hand, a 4% return is lower and the risk should be lower as well.

Q. Are there easy ways to spot safe versus risky investments?

A. If the average return is high, then the risk is generally higher. It's as simple as that! Beyond that, read all the information available on the investment, seek expert views and do lots of homework so you understand the investment before you put your money on the line. But remember, if the return sounds too good to be true then it probably is too good to be true. High return investments may work in the short term, but can also fail, and generally the longer you hold them, the more riskier they are.

Q. Other risks?

A. Apart from dodgy advisers, misleading advertisements and prospectuses, be mindful of how inflation affects your investments.

Q. How does inflation affect my investments?

A. Inflation undermines the real payoff from your investment. If inflation is 4% and you're getting a return of 6%, then your real payoff is only 2%. Smarties would not lock into a long-term bank deposit with a fixed interest rate if they thought inflation was going to rise. Of course, if you were given the inside tip that inflation was expected to fall, then locking in would be a clever ploy. Unfortunately, banks have experts who give them similar tips, however, these guys and gals can get it wrong. Of course, inflation is low now but might not always be the case. So remember this inflation insight.

Q. Any other traps?

A. Yes, there is a little thing called tax, which can have a rather significant impact on your long-run return.

Q. What can I do about it?

A. Well, start reading tax advice books in your spare time (which can be taxing!) and talk to an accountant or a financial planner. One thing is for certain: the longer you leave it, the more likely you're passing up money saving and wealth building opportunities. These can look small over a week or even a year but over 10 or 40 years, they could add up to a small fortune. (I'll give some tax tips later in the book in Chapter 11.)

Q. What's the most important thing I should know?

A. That's simple! You should know what you have to save each year to get what you want when you retire or when you want to use the end-product of your saving and investing. It's knowing your money goals. That's why you have to start becoming money smart or else become smart enough to go to someone who'll do it for you. If you 'put your head in the sand' when it comes to money matters, you could wind up with a shocking kick in your rear-end later in life.

Q. How do I work out that goal and how do I make it happen?

A. Keep reading this book!

06 LET'S BECOME A BUYER OF STOCKS

"If nothing changes, nothing changes, so just do it!"

Some wise guy!

I want to cut through the detail and simply tell you now what rich people know about the share market that we all should know. This won't be a long chapter with piles of information, but it will get straight to the point on how you get richer by understanding the share market.

I want you to get richer and I want to show you a simple, albeit slow and low risk way to do this. So here we go...

Look at this chart (my favourite chart) over the page and watch $10,000 turn into $471,593 in just under 40 years!

Follow the black line as it shows how $10,000 became $471,593 one year after the Global Financial Crisis saw stock markets crash by 50%! That $10,000 grew, despite its many ups and downs to eventually accumulate to $471,593!

INVESTMENT PERFORMANCE: 30 JUNE 1970 - 31 JULY 2009

Total returns for a $10,000 investment with no acquisition costs or taxes and all income reinvested

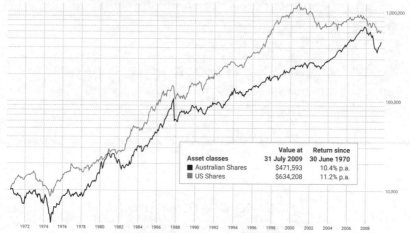

Asset classes	Value at 31 July 2009	Return since 30 June 1970
■ Australian Shares	$471,593	10.4% p.a.
■ US Shares	$634,208	11.2% p.a.

Source: Andex Charts Pty Ltd/ Vanguard Investments Australia Ltd.

Let me explain what you're looking at. I know the numbers on each axis are tiny but we just couldn't get them any bigger. It's your bank account that I want to get bigger anyway! Imagine you put your $10,000 into something special that gave you the top 200 companies in Australia in one virtual 'stock'. Let's say this 'stock' was priced at $10 so you bought 1,000 of them. The stock's value went up and down and your $10,000 grew and fell but see how the black line over time continued rising. This line shows you what stock markets do over time — they rise and fall but on a rising trend, and you can make money out of that!

How could you do this? You could buy this 'stock' called an exchange traded fund (or ETF that I explain on the next page), with special codes such as VAS, STW or IOZ, through an online broker such as nabtrade. If you don't have an account, see page 82 at this end of this chapter where I show you a step-by-step process for setting up an online account.

DO NOW

Once you've set up your account, consider putting in as little as $1,000 and see it grow to a big number over 40 years! Of course, you can get your money out earlier and the chart opposite shows there's a pretty good pay off even after 10 years.

You can even start investing with as little as $500. This is the minimum amount of shares you can initially purchase in any listed company. Share prices vary enormously, from over $200 a share to as low as a fraction of a cent. Therefore, the number of shares in any company you buy depends on how much you have to invest and its share price. You'll also need to pay brokerage (i.e. a fee to the broker) on each share transaction.

Nabtrade charges brokerage at a flat rate of $14.95 for transactions up to $5,000 in value; $19.95 for transactions from $5,001 to $20,000 in value; and 0.11% of the value if that's over $20,000. There's no stamp duty or other transaction costs, and you only pay brokerage when you actually have been successful with buying shares you want.

CHECK IT OUT

Between 1970 and 2009 (one year after the GFC stock market crash that cut many investors' total funds in half!) $10,000 invested in something like IOZ had grown to $471,593!

Q. What are VAS, STW or IOZ?

A. These are the ticker codes or stock market codes for an ETF. IOZ was created by a company called iShares. You can look up IOZ on the Internet, say on the Yahoo Finance website and you'll see it has a unit price. Think of it like a stock price. If the stock market for our top 200 companies goes up, the unit price on IOZ goes up and vice versa. If the unit price was $50 in the morning and ended up at $52 by the afternoon, you would've made $2 on $50, or 4% in a day! VAS and STW are similar products.

Q. What's an ETF?

A. This is a fund of, say stocks, put together by a company, such as Blackrock (which owns iShares) or Vanguard. You can buy or sell the units in the fund on the Stock Exchange, which is why it's called an Exchange Traded Fund. IOZ for example, has the top 200 companies in it and tracks the S&P/ASX 200 Index.

Q. What's this Index?

A. When you hear on the radio or TV that the stock market was up 1% on the day, the money journalist is usually quoting this Index of our biggest 200 companies on the Stock Exchange. In this case if you owned IOZ, you'd be 1% richer minus a small fee charged annually. If over the year the stock market was up 10%, you'd be just short of 10% richer.

In 2017, my company created an exchange traded product (ETP) where we look for the best dividend-paying companies in Australia. It's called the Switzer Dividend Growth Fund and has the ticker code of my nickname — SWTZ! This has been set to pay slightly higher dividends than IOZ because we have set this as a goal. We might get a little less capital growth than IOZ because we want more income for our unit holders.

Q. What's the difference between income and capital gain (or growth)?

A. When the stock price goes up, that's what you call a capital gain. If you bought a stock for $10 and it went to $18 and then you sold it, you'd pay capital gains tax on the $8 a share you profited over the time of holding the stock. (If you don't sell it, you don't pay tax.) If you hold it for over a year the capital gains tax is halved. This is called the capital gains tax discount.

When it comes to stocks, income is the dividend you receive. You pay tax on this dividend at your marginal tax rate or the rate of tax relevant to your income tax bracket.

By the way, capital gain is treated as income by the Tax Office. Most shares pay dividends. Some don't but these are the ones that often have the potential for big capital gains or losses. They are often more risky stocks but can be more exciting!

Also, if you buy shares and lose money, you can use those losses to offset any capital gain you've made on other assets. If you made $10,000 capital gain or profit on some shares that you've sold but you lost $4,000 on others you sold, you'd only pay capital gains tax on $6,000. And if you'd held them for a year or more, you'd only pay tax on half of that amount or $3,000. By the way, you can use your losses from shares any other time in the future. It's a loss you can use to soften the blow of tax you might have to pay! Note you only pay capital gains tax when you sell the shares.

Remember a stock market goes up and down, as the chart on page 76 shows, but it does so on a rising trend. In the short term the trend might be negative but nearly every 10 years, there are generally seven to eight years of rises for stock markets and this gets magnified the more 10-year periods you remain invested. Look at the black line on my favourite chart and see the big five dips, which were market crashes, but the rising trend kept re-emerging.

What I've described is an easy way to get into the stock market. If someone had followed my advice in early 2009 and bought something like IOZ (or other ticker codes e.g. VAS or STW), they would've made over 120% on their investment and this hasn't been a great period for Aussie stocks!

Using ETFs is a simple way to get exposure to the stock market. Great fund managers try to beat the Index but most don't. Many do just as well as this important benchmark or Index but personally, I like a mix of ETFs and actual fund managers who invest in a special way to give me diversification. For example, I use fund managers to invest overseas in companies such as Facebook, Amazon, Netflix, Google and Tencent.

Q. Can you tell me a bit about the size of the Australian share market?

A. Our share market is home to some of the world's leading resource, finance and healthcare companies. More than 2,200 companies are listed on our main exchange, the Australian Securities Exchange (ASX). The total value of companies on the ASX adds up to over $1.5 trillion and is ranked around 15th in the world by market size. Each trading day around $5 billion of shares are traded on the ASX and a second exchange, Chi-X.

Q. How do I know what's going on inside a company whose shares I might want to buy?

A. An ASX-listed company must adhere to strict rules relating to 'continuous disclosure', which means the company must advise the market on any material change in its state of affairs as soon as that happens, and comply with principles relating to corporate governance. If there's any major development that could affect its share price, the company must inform officials at the ASX. This is good news because you learn what's going on within a company, provided you show interest in your stock purchases.

Q. So who owns all these shares?

A. Individual Australian investors, superannuation funds, including self managed superannuation funds (SMSFs) and large retail and industry super funds, institutions and offshore investors. Around 31% of adult Australians own shares (one of the highest rates in the world), while many more Australians own shares indirectly through their super fund.

Q. So how do I become one of these owners?

A. Read the information over the page about setting up a trading account. But read this book so you have a sensible strategy in place before you go off trading shares without the required knowledge.

For now, what I've shown you is a good way to get started with wealth generation to put you on the road to riches. I want you to read the next chapter so you'll learn how to play the share market with knowledge. I want you to learn from the world's greatest investor Warren Buffett, often called the Oracle of Omaha, because that's where he lives. Buffett knows hot to buy stocks the way a true professional, not an amateur, does. It's time to give up amateur ways.

If someone had followed my advice in early 2009 and bought something like IOZ (or other ticker codes e.g. VAS or STW), they would've made over 120% on their investment and this hasn't been a great period for Aussie stocks!

HOW TO BECOME A BUYER OF STOCKS
Follow these steps and it's easy!

To invest in shares, you need to use a stockbroker. When most people think of a stockbroker, they think of Leonardo DiCaprio from *The Wolf of Wall Street*, but in real life it's far more boring.

DO NOW

There are two different types of stockbrokers:

1. Full service brokers (who will give you advice about what to buy and sell)

2. 'Execution only' brokers. An execution only broker is essentially an online broker linked to a bank account where you can buy and sell stocks yourself. These are normally very easy to set up, and very cheap to use.

One of the main online brokers in Australia is nabtrade. It's free to set up an account. In about 10 minutes, you can start buying shares all over the world.

I asked Tom, one of the guys in my team to create a simple guide to develop a trading account to buy stocks. This is what he came up with:

To create a nabtrade account you'll need:

- Your basic contact details.
- A valid email address.
- A tax file number (you can set up an account without a TFN, but you'll be slugged extra tax if you leave this out so it's better to have this upfront).
- A valid driver's licence or passport.

How to set up an account

Now you have this information and your identification in front of you, here's what you do:

1. Visit nabtrade.com.au/onboarding.
2. Select the account you want to open and click "next". If you're new to shares and are investing in your own name, it's likely an 'individual' account.
3. Select 'With a Cash Account' on the next page, then continue.
4. If you're an existing NAB customer, you can login with your Internet Banking details. Otherwise you can create a new account from scratch.
5. Fill out the details and submit. You'll be sent temporary login details that you'll update the first time you log in.

Yes, setting up an account where you can buy and sell shares is this easy! So now let's go to the next step.

How to make an investment

1. Login at nabtrade.com.au and click 'trade' in the top right.
2. Enter the details of the company or fund you want to buy. For example, you could search 'Switzer' and select the option that appears.
3. Select 'Buy' as the action.
4. Under 'Amount type', select 'Value', then enter how much you want to invest.
5. Under 'Order type', select 'Market', and leave 'Duration' as 'Good until Cancelled'
6. Click 'Review order' to check the details.
7. Click 'Submit'.

Congratulations, you now have the ability to be a fully-fledged share investor! However the last thing I want for you is to start trading without knowledge. Share trading is not gambling. You shouldn't take a 'punt' on a stock.

Q. OK so I now have my nabtrade account open but I'd like to know a few more things. For example, how do shares trade?

A. The ASX runs an electronic trading platform where brokers lodge orders to buy or sell shares. Each listed company has its own unique stock code, which is usually 3 letters in length e.g. BHP's stock code is 'BHP', Commonwealth Bank's is 'CBA', Woolworths' is 'WOW'. As I mentioned before, the stock code is also called the "ASX code" or "ticker".

Orders to buy or sell are arranged by a listed company, and a trade occurs when a buyer's price (known as a "bid") and a seller's price (known as an "offer") overlap. If the bid price is $2 and the seller's offer price is $2.20, then nothing happens. If they match, bingo! That stock is sold.

Q. So that means the shares are mine?

A. Because there are hundreds of participants in the market, there can be several bids or offers at the same price. If the bid price overlaps with the offer price, then as many bids and offers are matched and traded so that the quantity of shares bought is equal to the quantity of shares sold. Orders are arranged on a price/time priority and date stamped. When prices overlap and orders are traded, the earliest order has priority over the next earliest, and is filled in full before the next order is allocated any shares.

Q. What happens if my trade is successful?

A. Following a transaction, you'll be sent a contract note from your broker confirming the details of the transaction and settlement arrangements. In Australia, shares settle on a "transaction date plus 2 working days' basis" ("T+2"), meaning that settlement occurs 2 working days' after the transaction date. So, if you trade on a Monday, settlement occurs on the Wednesday. If you trade on a Thursday, settlement occurs on the following Monday. On the settlement date, buyers pay the proceeds (via their brokers, and their bank accounts are debited), while sellers receive the proceeds. The register of shareholders is updated to record the details of the new owner.

Q. How do I place an order?

A. There are two types of orders: a 'limit' order and a 'market' order.

A 'limit' order is an instruction to buy or sell at a particular price. If the market never trades at that price, because your buy price is too low or your sell price is too high, then the order will never take place.

A 'market' order is an instruction to buy or sell at the best available price. Provided the market is open and trading, it should go through immediately. When your broker receives a 'market' buy order, they will (electronically) find the seller at the best available price and purchase the number of shares you want. You'll pay the price the seller was offering.

You also need to specify the number of shares you want to buy (it can be any number provided that it amounts to at least $500 in value), or in the case of a sell, the number of shares you want to sell. You can't sell more shares than you own, but you don't have to sell your entire holding – you can sell any number. Or you can specify a "dollar" amount (say $2,000) and the broker will calculate the maximum number you can buy.

An order can be:

- 'good for day', which means it will automatically be cancelled if it's outstanding at the end of the trading day;

- 'good til cancelled', which means it will be in the market until it is executed or you cancel it;
- 'good until date', which means it will be in the market until it is executed or automatically cancelled at the close on the date you nominated.

Q. So where's the record of my purchase kept?

A. Shareholder records are maintained on a secure, centralised electronic register accessed by brokers and share registries acting on behalf of listed companies. This is operated by the ASX to clear and settle transactions and is known as CHESS.

Q. What do I receive as a shareholder?

A. After you complete your first trade, you'll receive a contract note from nabtrade, a CHESS holding statement from the ASX, and a welcome pack from the company. The latter will invite you to provide

- details of a bank account for any dividend payments;
- your tax file number or exemption (which is not compulsory); and
- communication preferences for receiving notices, annual reports and other information from the company.

If the company operates a dividend re-investment plan, you'll also receive information on the plan and how you can elect to participate.

A dividend re-investment plan means your dividends, rather than being taken as cash, can be used to purchase more shares in the company in question. These shares can be bought at a discount to the market price in some circumstances.

As a shareholder, you'll be entitled to attend the company's annual general meeting (and any general meetings) and vote on resolutions, including the election of directors and the remuneration arrangements for key officers. You can also vote electronically ahead of the meeting or appoint a proxy, so someone else can attend and vote on your behalf. You can also choose to receive a copy of the company's annual report and other important information. In essence if you've bought shares in BHP, Telstra or Woolworths, you own a part of those companies now!

MY TIP

If you want to grow your wealth to become richer, you have to do things differently. So if you haven't done this already, go and get yourself a trading account right now! Don't put it off. As the Nike commercials say: "Just do it!"

DO NOW

I want to change you! Remember the quote at the beginning of this chapter: If nothing changes, nothing changes, so just do it!

MY OTHER TIP

Read all this book and be committed to changing your amateur ways when it comes to money, building wealth and becoming richer to end up being an informed income grower.

TIP

Now it's time to read the next chapter about the "rich stuff" that smarties know about investing in shares.

07 SHARES PLAYED WISELY CAN MAKE YOU RICH

"...be fearful when others are greedy
and greedy when others are fearful."

Warren Buffett, the Oracle of Omaha

Okay it's time for me to share with you the actual stock-playing money secrets that can make you richer than you would be if you rely on the usual money-making plan that most of us rely on. I compare that 'plan' (which isn't really a plan or a wealth-building strategy) to the old joke of the Irish minesweeper who tippy toes through the minefield with his fingers in his ears! (For PC readers, I'm of Irish heritage so I can do Paddy jokes!) Or else it could be the eureka approach to getting rich, where you work hard and hope one day you'll make a nice discovery in your bank balance! And sure, some people get lucky with their homes they bought for $54,000 in 1979 in Paddington, Sydney, which is now worth over $2 million but there are only limited numbers of these properties with lucky people inside them.

GET RICH DAILY WITH SHARES

A few years back, I emceed a conference in Dubai where US-based John Maxwell was the keynote speaker. (I guess by now you can see that I do a lot of speaking both here and overseas! It's a tough job but someone has to do it!) I was knocked out by the calibre of this guy's message. He wrote one of my favourite books — *The 21 Irrefutable Laws of Leadership* — and it's a life-changer if you read it and want to boost your leadership skills. John showed me that, while I was building a successful business and employing more and more people, I had one weak-suit: I'd never really worked on something called leadership! I did it but I wasn't benchmarking myself and getting better at it.

It might come naturally to a few but Maxwell says leadership can be learnt.

John argues you don't learn leadership in a day but daily! I say the same applies to wealth — if you get it right by the day, over time, compound interest (see page 70 for an explanation) will work its magic and yes, you will end up wealthier.

Maxwell explains that his biggest lesson was when a mentor asked him what his self-improvement programme was. Like many of us, he admitted he didn't have one.

He makes a strong point that leading others starts with self-leadership and being committed to a self-improvement plan is step one. As a financial planner, I always make the point to clients that we have turned their money chaos life into one that is characterised by order.

This whole book is all about helping you to take control, to lead yourself to a better career, a more valuable business and a greater pool of money building in your bank account, your property investments and super fund. This is how YOU can get richer!

PERFECT PROCESSES PRODUCE POWERFUL PERFORMANCES

Maxwell is not a money expert but he shared with me a great wealth building story that shows how having the right processes helps you build income beyond your wildest dreams.

Lance Armstrong in his 'mea culpa' with Oprah Winfrey after being exposed as a drug-user, continually referred to "it's a process" and this is something out and out champions understand. Now I know it could be argued that Armstrong was an out and out champion cheat, but it still shows that whatever he does he will always strive to win, no matter what has to be done to make it happen.

With the Oprah interview, he was engaged in a process to win in trying to change the public's attitude towards him. Now that will be a big challenge but I bet at some time, maybe after a confession book, or after dedicating his life to helping other athletes to not make the same mistakes he made, Armstrong will gain some acceptance.

If he does achieve this, it will be put down to the process he put in place to change peoples' opinions of him. When that happens, (if it does), he will win.

By the way, Armstrong invested $100,000 in a little known company in 2009 called Uber. It is believed that his investment is valued now at $20 million in 2018!

SEEKING THE BEST-IN-BREED STRATEGY FOR STOCKS

The difference between ordinary employees and super ones, between average entrepreneurs and great performers, money strugglers successful wealth-builders and park players and top athletes is all about the process.

Maxwell told me about Anne Scheiber, who was a 101-year -old New Yorker who lived in a beaten-up studio apartment in Manhattan. The rent was $400 a month and she lived on social security and a small pension. She had worked for the Inland Revenue Service (like our tax office) and had retired in 1943 and despite having a law degree, she was only paid $3,150 a year.

She was regarded as a very thrifty person and even went to the New York public library to read the *Wall Street Journal* once a week. Despite this humble life, Ms. Scheiber left the Yeshiva University some $22 million! How did this lady build such a fortune? One day at a time, using a damn good process!

When Anne retired in her early 50s, she had $5,000 saved, which she ploughed into a quality company, Schering-Plough. She re-invested her profits back into the company. When she passed away, she had 128,000 shares of Schering-Plough valued at $7.5 million. Clearly, she held other companies too.

Her process was simple — buy quality companies, especially when the market fell, which made them easier to buy. She re-invested her dividends and stayed in for the long haul.

She was driven by her process and it was a good one — the results proved that — and she won big time by repeating this process over a number of quality investments.

As you set out your plans to build wealth, whether it be for your career, business or your investments, the critical question you have to ask yourself is — do I have the right process?

This leads to the next logical question, which is — how do you get the right process?

You could benchmark yourself off the best in breed. That's why I, as an employer of 50 plus and owner of a number of businesses, have read books such as Richard Branson's *Losing My Virginity* and Walter Isaacson's biography of Steve Jobs.

These guys had the right processes to create standout businesses. Obviously, tennis legend Serena Williams has the right process and so does Roger Federer — their results prove it.

LEARNING FROM LEGENDS

For building wealth, reading books (like *The Snowball* by Alice Schroeder) on the likes of Warren Buffett, regarded as one of the best investors of all time, could be a start or you could read personal investment books from a point of view of becoming your own financial adviser.

Others have used professional and trustworthy financial advisers to help construct their plan, which ultimately is the process that builds your wealth.

If you can write down your goals, which is the starting point for success, then follow that up with how you're going to achieve those goals. This is the critical process that I think is the difference between winning and losing. I first suggested this way back in chapter 1 and we created a page for you to write down your goals, and to do a SWOT on "you" on page 17.

In business, the process has to be about satisfying customers; for employees, it's about understanding the goals of the business and being the best contributor you can be to help kick those goals. In 2012, I shared with our subscribers to my *Switzer Report* (for investors and those investing in stocks and other financial assets), a wealth building process where I suggested a portfolio of quality Aussie company names that have a history of paying great dividends.

The goal was simple — let's try and make 6-7% on dividends and if we get capital gain that will be a bonus. That portfolio across 2012 returned over 20%!

I had no control over what the market did, what Mario Draghi, the central bank boss in Europe, said or how fast China grew but I could control the companies that my money and my clients' money went into.

And if we didn't get capital gain growth in any one year, we would have got 7% in dividends. If the market went down and these companies became very cheap, I would've recommended buying more, just like Anne Scheiber did.

When the process has been proven, you can withstand disappointing results because you know one day that things will change and your time-tested process will come through.

The trick is for you to discover the right process and think and invest long term.

In 2014, I spoke at a property conference in Brisbane with the likes of John McGrath, estate agent entrepreneur and Chris Gray from the old Sky Business programme *Your Property Empire*. Reality says that a million dollars in super will give you a comfortable retirement. A couple of million will give you a great retirement. Anything more is a bonus — a really good bonus.

The MC was an unbelievably excitable guy who got everyone up dancing before the speakers let loose. I saw one lady ignoring his antics, instead browsing through *The Courier Mail* until I went on stage.

Looking at her and the MC and the crowd buying into his enthusiasm, I recognised that he was a 'take you out of your comfort zone' kind of guy. This woman just couldn't get out of her own comfort zone

I believe success is based on continually looking at the uncomfortable things that might be holding you back. What might they be?

Try the following list to see if you have a discomfort zone avoidance issue:

- Laziness.
- Fear.
- You won't pay for help.
- You won't be taught.
- You hate change.
- Procrastination.
- You won't read or pursue media that will show you what you don't know.

Back to Brisbane and I congratulated the people who showed up to the conference on the basis they had beaten many of the hold-back factors that explain why people are not successful.

SEARCH FOR THE RIGHT PROCESS

I also warned them about taking short-cuts in trying to build a million-dollar-making portfolio. I even suggested that they learn how to beat the obstacles that are holding them back by listing all the challenges that are hurting their progress, from hardest at the top to easiest at the bottom.

You need to create a system to beat the easiest challenges and work your way through until you beat all your challenges. John Maxwell says we have to embrace the Law of Process and he shares two great stories to prove the value of having processes that lead to success.

This is the work you should be doing daily, as you don't build wealth in a day but daily. (Have I said that before?!) Champion boxers don't really become champions in the ring, they're merely recognised there.

The story of US president Theodore Roosevelt is one that really underlines my point. The British historian Hugh Brogan said of him: "The ablest man to sit in the White House since Lincoln;

the most vigorous since Jackson; the most bookish since John Quincy Adams." That's huge praise.

Roosevelt was born weak and sickly but was smart so his father told him that he had to "get physical" or he was done for. He committed to a daily routine of weights and would do everything from ice skating to horse riding to boxing.

He was a cowboy in the Wild West and in the cavalry in the Spanish-American War. He was bigger than life and even when he died, he had a book in his bed. A close colleague remarked after he died: "Death had to take him sleeping, for if Roosevelt had been awake, there would have been a fight."

Like so many impressive leaders, this guy was right into self-improvement — physical and mental — but more importantly, it was a commitment to getting better daily.

This is exactly what I told the audience about building wealth through real estate. The same applies to shares — you have to become a professional. You need to give up amateurish ways and be on the constant lookout for knowledge that will give you a competitive advantage.

You don't become a millionaire property owner in one day, but daily. And the value of your assets will grow with the body of knowledge you accumulate.

IMPORTANT

Being a success is hard work combined with a really sound process. It starts with a daily commitment to self-improvement.

If you can't do that, then accept you will be an average performer, unless you get lucky!

"I know I keep repeating how essential it is to have the right mindset in order to build wealth and I won't stop because it is fundamentally important if you want financial independance."

INVEST IN KNOWLEDGE: CHANGE THE ATTITUDE CHANGE THE BANK BALANCE!

You're never too young or too old to learn, especially when it comes to investing in stocks. Watching the period after the GFC crash of the market in 2007-09 and the associated daily work I've done monitoring the gradual comeback of stocks and then communicating what I've learnt with followers of my daily column on www.switzer.com.au, it's clear there are fundamental principles all investors must learn.

The big moments in history of the GFC clearly were the collapse of Bear Stearns, Lehman Brothers, the US Government bail-outs of the likes of the world's biggest insurer AIG, the world's biggest bank Citigroup, most of the US car industry and Ben Bernanke's big gambles of quantitative easing, which means that the US Central Bank increased the money supply, which results in lower interest rates and helps lending.

This was all discredited by conservative economists who wanted to cut spending to kill the growth of debt. But the likes of Barack Obama and Bernanke took the lessons of economist J.M. Keynes, who in the 1930s Great Depression recommended policies "spend and prosper" when it came to serious economic collapses.

And it worked, if you judge that by the comeback of the US stock market's Dow Jones Index, which hit a low of around 7000 in 2008-09 and now is in the 25,000 neighbourhood at the time of writing in 2019! And even Europe eventually adopted a less austere approach to fixing their economies – green shoots of growth sprouted and the stock markets on the Continent surged. Mario Draghi, the European Central Bank boss, was the never-too-old-to-learn-hero in this case and in doing so, he'll always be remembered for the "whatever it takes" war cry, which helped build confidence in Europe and set it on a course to recovery.

The most memorable event in this long, dramatic saga involved stock market legend, Warren Buffett. In 2008, Buffett put $5 billion on the table and lent it to Goldman Sachs. That was huge. It was symbolic and inspirational. Buffett was not only punting on Goldman Sachs he was backing capitalism, the potential of the USA and a belief in the F.D. Roosevelt line that "all there was to fear was fear itself."

Sure, he could have been wrong, but this guy was and is the master valuer of a company, so I was prepared to take his valuation of the USA and run hard on the belief that the global economy would avoid a Great Depression. So great companies, such as CBA, Westpac, Telstra and the like, were worth investing in.

In 2018, our All Ordinaries Accumulation Index (AOAI) hit an all-time high, despite the fact that we were a long way off our all-time high for the index itself. What is an index? It's a way to measure rising or falling prices. The share prices of the top

TECHNICAL

200 companies are measured daily in the S&P/ASX 200 index. If the index rises 2% in a day, it means the collective rises and falls in share prices of the top 200 companies in total rose by 2% on that day. By the way, the difference between the AOAI and the All Ords is the important reason to invest — dividends. So the Accumulation Index adds in dividends to capital gain from rising share prices — it's a total return index and is more important for an investor trying to build wealth.

(Let me remind you that the history of stock markets tells us that the All Ords returns about 10% per annum over a 10-year period and half of that return comes from dividends. You could have some bad and negative years in those 10 years but the good ones, and the fact that there are more of them, help push up that return over a decade.) It's like a landlord who makes money long-term from rising house prices as well as rents, which are pocketed regularly. Share prices can go up and down big time but dividends have a great inclination to trend higher and, as a group, they don't tend to collapse.

CBA TEACHES YOU A LOT

The graph below shows you what a quality stock market performing company such as CBA can deliver with dividends.

In 1992, the Commonwealth Bank's first year as a public company, it paid a total dividend of 40 cents a share. By 2018, this had risen to 431 cents (yes, $4.31) a share! Note that dividends kept on rising with only one small dip because of the GFC in 2009.

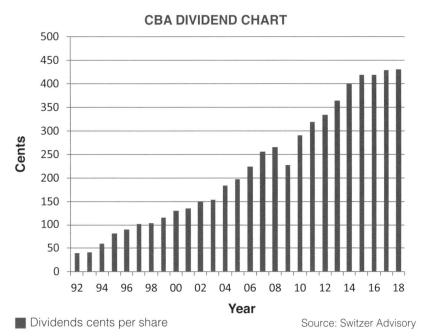

CBA DIVIDEND CHART

■ Dividends cents per share   Source: Switzer Advisory

You really get to understand the power of dividends when you see what would have happened if you put your money into a 10% government bond in 1992. See the next graph over the page.

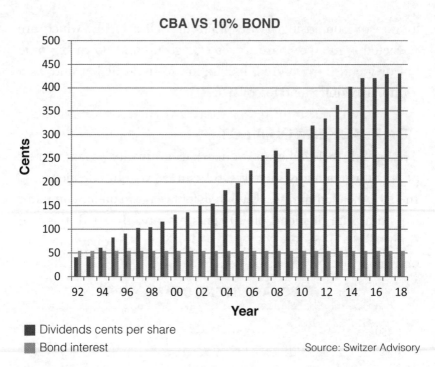

CBA VS 10% BOND

Year

■ Dividends cents per share
■ Bond interest

Source: Switzer Advisory

The lighter line of bars shows you would have received the steady return of 10% in bonds but after 1994 you were miles better off having your money in stocks that pay dividends. By the way, over that time, CBA's share price also went from $5.40 to around $80 today!

Let's now look at the big picture. The All Ords hit its best level on 1 November 2007 at 6853.6. Even by mid 2019 we hadn't passed this all-time high. But with dividends included, anyone who lost 50% of their wealth in the GFC stock market crash, would now be back in the black, thanks to dividends.

Remember, history shows that a good portfolio of stocks that's as good as the All Ords Index should return 10% a year over a 10-year period, where you'll see two or three bad years. But the good ones make up for the disappointing ones. And half of this

10% is dividends! (I know I've said this before but I want to ram home the message.)

DON'T IGNORE THE DIVIDEND

IMPORTANT

Of course, the reason the AOAI (All Ords Accumulation Index)was in all-time high territory for the first half of 2019 was because dividends are so important. A few years back, Rudi Filapek-Vandyck from FNArena told me a lady bailed him up in Melbourne to complain about a stock tip he'd given that had only risen 2% in two years. He said to her: "What about the 7% dividend it has paid each year since the tip?"

She apologised but she showed how crazy we are as investors — 7% is a nice return and in fact she pocketed 8% a year with her capital gain over two years. And furthermore, with franking credits (I explain franking credits on page 141), that 7% could have been closer to 10%, especially if she had a self-managed super fund and she was retired!

DIVERSIFICATION: IT'S THE NAME OF THE GAME

IMPORTANT

One issue to consider when investing in shares is the level of diversification, i.e. how much of your portfolio is invested in different companies or stocks from different industries. When it comes to the stock market, the old adage "don't put all your eggs in one basket" (while not necessarily suitable for traders) resonates with investors. Some risks are specific to individual companies, while others are specific to particular industries or sectors.

HOW MY COLLEAGUE WHO STARTED COMMSEC INVESTS

Paul Rickard was the first CEO of CommSec and was recruited into the Stockbrokers Hall of Fame. This is how he invests in stocks after decades of buying and selling stocks and other wealth-building assets, such as bonds.

PAUL RICKARD:

My approach is based around some of the great investment adages: "time in the market rather than timing"; "don't put all your eggs in the one basket"; "let your profits run"; "the trend is your friend"; "your first loss is your best loss" and "there are only 3 things that move markets: greed, hope and fear".

I invest in all the major asset classes – shares, property and fixed interest – but have a bias for shares because the returns are tax effective, it's easier to diversify and I can always see what the market is doing, which makes it a little more "exciting".

With shares, I run a portfolio of stocks with representatives from most (but not all) of the major industry sectors. About 15-20 in number to give enough diversification. Five stocks doesn't provide enough diversification, while more than 25 stocks becomes too hard to manage.

In the Australian market, the dividend component is so important to long-term returns, particularly tax-adjusted returns, so I look for companies that have a track record of paying rising dividends. Strong and stable leadership is critical, as is culture, and a position of market leadership. This can be within a niche or industry vertical – but the company has to have a sustainable competitive advantage. For miners and other commodity companies, this means the least cost producer; for banks, the best technology and customer footprint; and for retailers, the category leader.

Then there is the question of price. As a value style investor, I want to pay a fair price. I assess this in the main by looking at the company's price/earnings (PE) ratio, a measure that expresses the current share price as a multiple of its forecast earnings. I look at how it stacks up relative to its industry peers and where it has traded historically. It is however, just a guide – more "art than science".

Like most investors, I fancy the idea of "buying low, selling high", but recognise that sometimes you just have to pay up to get set. I have given up trying to think that I can "buy at the bottom or sell at the top", however I can buy in dips and have learnt the hard way that trends go on longer than you expect. This also means letting your profits run.

I don't have time to do a lot of trading and I invest for the long term. If I do trade, cutting losses quickly becomes very important whereas for the investor, patience is a virtue. The market is cyclical, and because it is driven by such primal emotions, it over-reacts – both down and up. Over the long term, share prices rise, so by owning quality companies, I know they will come back. Junk companies, however, remain junk.

"I invest in all the major asset classes – shares, property and fixed interest – but have a bias for shares because the returns are tax effective, it's easier to diversify and I can always see what the market is doing..."

THIS IS HOW CHARLIE AITKEN PICKS STOCKS

Charlie was a renowned stockbroker who later started his Aitken Investment Management fund, which has attracted the money of some of Australia's richest investors. This is how Charlie picks stocks and invests:

CHARLIE AITKEN:

I'm the son of a fund manager. Unsurprisingly, I'm a fund manager and my two brothers also work in financial markets.

Some of my earliest memories are my Dad taking the three Aitken brothers for " Sunday drives" around Sydney. These drives were firstly, to give Mum a well-deserved break, and secondly for Dad to look at some of his investments.

Dad started the Perpetual Industrial Share fund and went on to be CEO of Perpetual. The investment standards that Dad introduced at Perpetual remain core today, based on quality businesses with low gearing.

Dad finished his investment career with the Fairfax Family Office, where he successfully oversaw their equity investments for 12 years, the star investment being CSL which he bought under $2. Nowadays, Dad is 83 years old but remains an active investor and active source of investment advice. He remains an excellent mentor.

Outside of my father, the second greatest influence on my approach to investing was reading a book titled *One up on Wall St, how to use what you already know to make money in the market* by the US fund manager, Peter Lynch.

Peter Lynch ran the Fidelity Magellan Fund and generated tremendous outperformance over two decades. The main premise of his book, which was written in 2000, was that the best investing ideas are the ones you can see with your own eyes in everyday life. I believe that is even more so in 2019 as the pace of change accelerates in all businesses.

The power of observation is our greatest investing advantage. With around 75% of GDP generated by "consumer spending", observing the consumption patterns in people's daily lives is the place to start the investment research process.

When I'm presenting to investors, I always say "you should look at the products and services your children and grandchildren use" as a guide to where companies are growing, and vice versa. The growth companies of today and the future are those companies whose products the generation younger embrace with vigour. The vast bulk of those products and services have a technology angle. The companies to avoid are the ones that the next generation shun.

"...look at the products and services your children and grandchildren use" as a guide to where companies are growing, and vice versa."

Outside of "getting out to find out" (observation), my investment process involves relentless reading. I want to know as much as I can about everything. I want the deepest general knowledge I can have, and I will source that information widely.

Then next step is to form a view of which sectors will outgrow GDP. The sectors to invest in are the ones that are growing at multiples of GDP. That is the macro tailwind you're looking for, where demand for goods and services in a given sector is a multiple of GDP. I call it structural growth.

Once I have identified "structural growth sectors" I then look for the no.1 or no.2 company globally, or both, with leverage to that structural growth theme. I start with the largest capitalisation stocks as they generally give you leverage to the structural growth theme with less risk. They also have the largest barriers to entry (moats) and generally the most experienced management teams and boards.

The final analysis is financial. I look at the investment arithmetic with an emphasis on Return on Equity (ROE), Return on Invested Capital (ROIC), Free Cash Flow (FCF), earnings per share growth over the next three years (3-year EPS G%), balance sheet and dividend payout ratio. Ideally, I want to own a company on a price-to-growth ratio (PEG ratio) of less than 1x.

The goal of the process is to own the best businesses in the best sectors in the world. Superior quality and long duration is never cheap. Not all companies were created equal. I will always pay a "premium" to Mr Market average P/E for a superior business with superior investment fundamentals.

The temptation to buy inferior companies is strong. Value arguments can be compelling. However, these companies are cheap for a reason: they are inferior and highly unlikely to be able to transform themselves to superior.

The temptation to over-trade portfolios is also strong. It's a temptation that must be resisted (sorry stockbroking friends).

In summary, I have a hybrid investment approach that represents the best I learned from my father, the common-sense of Peter Lynch, and what 25 years in markets has taught me.

"Own the very best businesses you can and own them for as long as you can."

THE ULTIMATE SAFE INVESTMENT STRATEGY

Let me tell you a story I shared with my subscribers to my *Switzer Report.* When people tell me the dividend play is over, I think of my 7% plus play and the best retirement plan I've ever seen from a guy who was an employee in a good job but his investment strategy was great.

He was always anti-property, though he retired with a nice three-bedroom apartment. He always bought great dividend paying stocks and retired with $5 million in his super! Buying great dividend-paying stocks when they looked cheap and reinvesting the dividends over 30 years can have surprisingly great returns.

Pre-GFC, his grossed up yield was around 10%. That's 10% on $5 million (or $500,000 a year) tax-free (the rules have changed and I explain this on page 118). The GFC in 2008 took the value of his shares down to around $4 million but his dividend yield was closer to 9% for 2009. In that year, he spent more time in France than usual and did that on a high Aussie dollar!

Now that's a retirement plan that tells me that dividend-paying stocks and knowledge about how markets work can be a great investment process or strategy. This book is about giving you the knowledge that the rich are given (or they pay for) to ensure they build and keep wealth. I'll look at this guy's wealth-building plan in more detail later in this chapter but here's his process in a nutshell:

1. He worked hard.
2. He had a savings plan.
3. He bought his own home.
4. He bought great dividend paying stocks of quality companies over many years.
5. He planned for an early retirement.
6. He lives off his dividends from his healthy stock portfolio.

5 OF THE BEST WEALTH BUILDING TIPS

After over 30 years of business and finance commentary and decades of metering out financial education, as well as advice to clients, these lessons are timeless, indisputable and worth burning onto your mental hard drive.

Lesson 1: Diversify

The first lesson is never be long on only one kind of asset — diversification is the name of the game. Sure, some high flyers will go long on shares only and I've done this in my self-managed super fund, but I have good exposure to property as well outside super. As your age, circumstances and appetite for risk change, you can change how you want to hold your wealth but having a nice mix makes a lot of sense.

Warren Buffett has said (and he might have been joking) that "diversification is for wimps." Let me say I prefer wimpy, cautious investment plays that, over time, turn out to be strong winners and performers.

Lesson 2: Invest long-term & know the asset

The second lesson applies to shares. If you want to be a thrill seeker and make lots of money from shares in a short time, you might do it, but you could also end up with the butt-plate out of your strides!

Shares are not just financial products that you can make or lose money on. They're also proof that you own a part of a publicly listed company. That's why you need to buy companies you want to own if you're a long-term wealth builder, as opposed to a short-term trader or speculator.

Many years ago, *The Times* in London had a competition between fund managers and some amateurs over a year to see who was the best stock picker. A chemist in a town called Luton won. When asked how he selected his companies, he said he visited the businesses, talked to staff and customers and made a judgment call on how good the business was. That's the clue — invest in good companies. They're often the ones you deal with on a daily basis, such as Woolworths, JB Hi-Fi, Origin, etc. Charlie Aitken is a huge advocate of this.

Lesson 3: Love dividends

My advice is for the long-term wealth builder. The unforgettable lesson is to become an owner of great companies that have a history of paying good to great dividends. History shows that over a 10, 15 and 20-year period, shares return around 10-12% and half of those returns come from dividends!

Cash and bank deposits might have averaged 5-6% until recently but there's no chance of capital growth for people who buy and hold these assets. That's why I recommend anyone wanting to create a good portfolio of shares to think about 20 great companies that pay dividends.

Buying 20 companies might mean you'll only have a 5% exposure to any one company, provided your money is allocated evenly. Some people might buy an Exchange Traded Fund (or ETF, which I explained in chapter 6 page 78) for the S&P/ASX 200 and that can be a good way to get exposure to both capital gain and dividends.

That said, I like a portfolio that's heavily skewed to great dividend payers. Sure, when the stock market takes off, dividend-stocks prices won't rise as rapidly as others that have been beaten up over the past few years — but they'll still go up, like all boats do with a rising tide.

You could buy your 20 stocks in different proportions as well, say matching the All Ords, or you could go top heavy on the best dividend payers. But I like having around 20 stocks so you aren't overexposed to one company.

This chart (I've shown you this previously but it now covers the extra period post the GFC) demonstrates why a good share portfolio over time is a winning strategy. It shows how $10,000 invested in 1970 into Australian shares has become $970,048. If you'd opted for US shares, the return would be $2,204,432. I rest my case.

INVESTMENT PERFORMANCE: 31 DEC 1969 - 30 APRIL 2019

Total returns for a $10,000 investment with no acquisition costs or taxes and all income reinvested

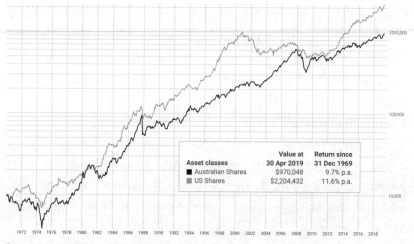

Asset classes	Value at 30 Apr 2019	Return since 31 Dec 1969
■ Australian Shares	$970,048	9.7% p.a.
■ US Shares	$2,204,432	11.6% p.a.

Source: Andex Charts Pty Ltd/ Vanguard Investments Australia Ltd.

"I like a portfolio that's heavily skewed to great dividend payers."

Peter Switzer

Lesson 4: Funds can do it for you

If you don't want to or don't think you're able to buy your own shares, investigate to find a fund or funds that suit you, your goals and your risk appetite. Go to websites such as www.superratings. com.au to find out the best super funds and at Morningstar.com.

 au you can compare investment funds. What you need to find are funds that have performed well over a long period and whose fees aren't exorbitant.

DO NOW

TOP 10 RETURNS FOR BALANCED OPTIONS
FOR 10 YEARS TO 30 APRIL 2019 (%)

Ranking	Superfund & investment option	10 years (% each year)
1	AustralianSuper - Balanced	9.5%
2	UniSuper Accum (1) - Balanced	9.4%
3	QSuper - Balanced	9.3%
3	TelstraSuper Corp Plus -Balanced	9.3%
3	Hostplus - Balanced	9.3%
3	CareSuper - Balanced	9.3%
7	Cbus - Growth (Cbus MySuper)	9.2%
7	Mercy Super - MySuper Balanced	9.2%
7	VicSuper FutureSaver-Growth (MySuper) option	9.2%
10	Sunsuper for Life - Balanced	9.1%

Source: SuperRatings

(Earlier I showed the best super funds but this was on a three-year basis. This table is for 10 years and the high returns reflect the fact that the stock market started to rebound in March 2009 and this captures returns since April 2009.)

Some investors and those running a self-managed super fund (SMSF) will set up a fund of funds, where they select fund managers to create an overall diversified fund and hopefully their combined expertise delivers above-index results. An SMSF can drive your costs down to 0.5% or lower, while typical super funds charge around 1%, so it can pay to become an SMSF investor.

Lesson 5: Dividends + Compounding = Wealth

To break with an investment strategy can be a risky play as I think it's generally very hard to time the market — and this is my final lesson, which has stood the test of time.

Once you have great dividend paying companies that are returning 7-8% per annum over a 10-year period, then your money doubles every 9-10 years! And while we can have some shocker years like we saw after the GFC, history tells us that good shares will deliver.

And when you add time to the compounding effect from dividend-paying shares, which can also bring capital growth as well, your money doubles and doubles and doubles!

When it comes to building a good nest egg, the former Kiwi supermodel Rachel Hunter, who was married to Rod Stewart, once said of a shampoo: "It won't happen overnight, but it will happen."

SHARES — IT'S NOT IN THE TIMING

One of the greatest challenges for anyone investing is to work out what your strategy is. For me, because I don't plan to retire for some time, I'm heavily exposed to the stock market but eventually I will become more conservative.

When you have a self-managed super fund, you must write down your investment strategy. We have an SMSF with one of our sons and we have a non-conservative approach to investing at the moment, so it's easy to construct a strategy that applies to all of us.

In a nutshell, our strategy is to be nearly fully invested in stocks, apart from a cash buffer to cover expenses for running the fund and any tax bills. Sometimes we let the cash reserves run up ahead of an expected sell off but this represents the toughest time for me as nominated chief investment officer. Generally, we buy dividend-paying stocks, as these are very reliable. And we buy good companies especially when the stock market dips.

I hate timing the market and prefer the old adage of "it's time in the market not timing the market" that brings great rewards on stock markets. That said, if you can time the market and then spend time in as well, you might pull off the double play.

Anyone who bought stocks for the first time in early March 2009 in the USA could be up over 300%, while Aussies could be up 130% including dividends.

This revelation about our investment strategy came because I received a letter from a subscriber to our *Switzer Report*, designed for those investing in stocks and for those running an SMSF. The subscriber wrote: "Knowing I'd be overseas for six weeks, and a little fearful of the 'cliff' implications, I liquidated my share investments mid Dec. Watching the market from afar, I'm now concerned that the ASX may accelerate further away from me. My dilemma is — do I now get back in or should I wait for a month or see how it may unfold in the USA? Whilst I realise you can't give specific advice, I would appreciate your general comment. I might add that my share proclivity is towards fundamentally sound good dividend Australian companies."

The subscriber's general strategy is sound and a bit like my strategy, but she's taken a punt on a big sell off and she was worried about a potential double whammy if she gets in and then there's a sell off.

Basically, I didn't know what the answer was but this is what history points to: January is good for stocks and it usually extends to March or even April. That's why there's that old market cliché — "sell in May and go away". If you tend to get in say November and ride the market until February or so, it can be a rewarding strategy but you will have the timing worries to keep you awake at night.

And in 2016, January until February 10 was a nightmare for stocks, so history doesn't repeat year in, year out.

TIMING STOCKS IS DAMN HARD

I always remember Paul Clitheroe's *Making Money* book showed a US study that showed timing the market is for mugs. The study by Professor William Sharpe of Stanford University in 1972 basically confirmed that if you changed your investments annually based on current market perceptions, you'd have to be right 70% of the time to increase your portfolio's value.

Paul looked at what you received if you remained fully invested between 1979 and 2006 and the average per annum return was 11.4%. However, if you were playing the 'in and out game' and you missed the 10 best days, your return dropped to 9%! If you missed the best 40 days, the return plummeted to a tick over 5%! By playing the long game, you saw a return from shares around 11% but if you tried to time the market and missed some of the big days on the stock market (which often happens when investors get fed up and run to cash), your returns fell markedly. The conclusion was 'time in the market' is better than trying to 'time the market'. Paul Rickard stresses this on page 102.

WHAT DOES A LONG-TERM PLAYER GET?

Russell/ASX research has shown that Aussie shares have returned 8.8% a year over the past 20 years, while cash returned 4.6%. And note this even covers the stock market crash of the GFC. Robin Bowerman of Vanguard Investments showed the median return of shares from 1950 to 2010 was 12.9% and the worst 20 years to February 2009 still came in with an 8.4% result!

What does all this prove? Well, provided your shares are quality ones that pay good dividends — you hover between what you get in cash or term deposits but you also get the chance for capital gain. When that happens, your returns can go to 8-10%.

I don't mind other assets such as property, cash, bond funds and term deposits but I stick like glue to stocks, long term.

INVESTING RIGHT

Way back in late 2008, a reader took me to task for being optimistic on stocks. He came from Canberra and gave me a real bollocking as a typical media or market flunky or worst still — a financial planner, just trying to drum up business.

Since March 2009, the S&P/ASX 200 index has gone up from 3145.5 to around 6600 (where it is at the time of writing), which is a gain of almost 109%. And if you add in dividends for 10 years of say 5%, we're up over 160%. And these OK returns were from a pretty subdued stock market from 2009-19.

By the way, that forgettable critic has never contacted me once to apologise or say, "Gee, I learnt something from that Switzer guy." Of course, I hope he did learn something but there are a lot of people who are out there refusing to learn important lessons about investing right.

Mind you, I think the guy who got stuck into me was an academic — he had such a snooty tone that reminded me of my days teaching Economics at the University of New South Wales. Not that I've ever been snooty!

Undoubtedly, there is no scientifically proven method for investing, so it's hard to be always right. But there are market truisms that can be relied upon to give you a good chance of investing successfully in the stock market.

PROPERTY OR SHARES?

A few years ago that friend I told you about (on page 107), who retired with $5 million in his super fund with a 10% yield tax-free, contacted me after a well-known property investor was on my old Sky Business programme talking about how he invested in the GFC.

This guy tipped $1.9 million into a property during the GFC, spent $600,000 on renovations and it's now 'valued' at $3.5 million. I'm sure many of my viewers would have thought he'd killed them with that return.

My mate's reaction to this story went like this: "If he'd done what I did and tipped his $1.9 million into, say, CBA during the GFC it would now be worth roughly $5 million and he would have had almost $1 million in income (franked). By the way, that is without tipping in another $600,000!"

But that's not all.

"If he'd done something similar with, say, Wesfarmers the story would be even better," he wrote. "It would be worth $5.7 million plus over $1 million in fully-franked income and a current dividend of $0.25 million."

Sure, you could argue that a crash could change these great numbers and property tends not to collapse by 50%, as stocks did in 2007-09. But some properties can. The Gold Coast actually saw some massive property price falls at the top end.

My friend is aware of what markets can do so he keeps a healthy cash balance in case his dividend returns drop significantly. But in reality, he and his wife find it difficult to spend $500,000 a year and if they were forced to live on $200,000 for a couple of years, they'd cope!

By the way, in 2008 with the GFC, his dividends dropped to $470,000 or so but in 2009 they were better than $500,000.

As you can see, he has a great investment strategy based primarily on buying great companies that have a solid history of paying dividends. He re-invests his dividends and knows some years his portfolio will do poorly compared to others exposed to big capital gaining stocks. But over a 10-year period, he'd average around a 10% return, which is superb.

As I said above, history has shown that stocks — a portfolio that at least matches the S&P/ASX 200 index — over a 10-year period will bring in about an 8-10% return but half of this is made up of dividends. So creating a portfolio of great dividend-payers pushes your average return up because you don't have those stocks that pay stingy dividends bringing your overall returns down.

And if you buy your stocks inside an SMSF, you pay only 15% tax pre-retirement and 0% tax when you retire, which can push up your dividend return by nearly 2%.

(I know I'm repeating myself but that's the old teacher in me. When it comes to getting a message across, I found that repeating important, memorable messages tended to stick.)

I argue that it's wise to get yourself a reliable investment strategy and stick to it. It would also be smart to link it to your financial goals and a plan that will make those goals or dreams come true. Imagine having a plan that didn't make you feel sick when a market crash came along. My mate actually took the GFC crash as an opportunity to buy more of the stocks he wants to hold until he turns up his toes. And because he bought the likes of CBA at low crash prices, he bumped up his percentage yield from his dividends. Now that's an investment plan we all have to have!

On real estate, I think it's also a great investment and in chapter 9 I'll show you how you should play property.

By the way, my friend's tax-free life has been affected by the new super rules that mean he can only have $1.6 million in his tax-free pension account. The balance of $3.4 million ($5 million minus $1.6 million) remains in his accumulation account where the earnings are taxed at 15%. If his spouse is in the super fund and they have been "smart", then she might also have $1.6 million in a tax-free pension account and only $1.8 million would have to go into the accumulation account.

Oh well, the tax treatment is tougher nowadays but his strategy for wealth-building using shares is still a ripper.

One last secret from my friend which I've already referred to is that he has built up a buffer of cash in case his dividends drop more than expected. Invariably, this builds up in the good stock market years and he then uses this to buy quality shares when markets crash and the buying is good.

Like me, my friend has been influenced by Warren Buffett — the Oracle of Omaha — who counsels us to:

TIP

"...be fearful when others are greedy and greedy when others are fearful."

Consider having a "virtual" tribe of investing mentors (in books, websites, on TV etc.), who you study and learn lessons from.

THE PROCESS OF MAKING & MANAGING MONEY

Making and managing your money is an ongoing process of embracing professionalism. It is self-leadership in the money arena and it could involve you becoming your own virtual financial planner or else you farm out the work to a professional. Either way, it has to be done to seriously build your wealth.

Let me retell you that true story you should never forget.

I introduced you to Anne Scheiber earlier in the chapter. Recall that she lived on social security in New York in an old apartment for $400 a month. She had been an IRS employee — that's the tax office in the USA. Everyone thought she was poor but when she died at 101 years of age she left the Yeshiva University US$22 million!

When she retired from the IRS in 1943 she had $5,000 in savings, which she put into quality stocks. She kept them, re-invested the dividends and kept building her wealth.

Remember that I said that Anne committed to John Maxwell's Law of Process, where she had a plan to build wealth — it was a good one — and she stuck to it, building up her wealth to $22 million, which she left to Yeshiva. That's commitment!

GETTING THE PLAN & PROCESS RIGHT

The building blocks of making and managing money can be put down to a simple process, which most people can't stick to. That's why they find it hard to build wealth.

You could start with goals such as $1 million in your super fund, a house paid off and a rental property. Then you work out how much you have to save each week to invest to make your goal happen. This gives you a savings target. To find the money, you have to do a budget to see what income you have and how you spend it. If the budget shows you

IMPORTANT

that you're not making the savings target, then you have to get more income or cut your expenses.

You might have to get a second job (or a better one) or try to cut your spending by say 10%. You might become a smarter-shopper and this could deliver the savings.

Once you have the savings target mastered, you then need the plan. This plan could be constructed by a professional financial adviser or you could do it yourself — just like Anne Scheiber.

If you're not an expert in investment matters, I'd recommend finding an accountant to help you with tax issues that could help you achieve your goals (you can check out some tax tips in chapter 11) and a financial planner for the investment strategy. A good stockbroker could also help or you could read and do plenty of research to construct your own plan.

Too many people think it's all too hard and they won't pay for help so nothing happens — this is false economy. If the goals are important, such as sending your kids to private schools, looking after your family to a standard you want or just being able to retire early, then you have to get a plan and be committed to it. Here I go again but writing down your goals on page 17 is the key to your financial strategy.

There are many ways to build wealth — buying income-paying stocks, accumulating great rental properties, borrowing and using the tax system and a whole lot more. But the first step is to work out your goals and then move to get a plan in place.

"Remember, you don't grow wealth in a day but daily!"

MORE LESSONS FROM THE LEGENDARY WARREN BUFFET!

Warren Buffett is the Michael Jordan or Don Bradman of stock market investing. Here are some of his famous quotes which are lessons in their own right:

- Rule No.1: Never lose money.
- Rule No.2: Never forget rule No.1.
- Risk comes from not knowing what you're doing.
- It's only when the tide goes out that you discover who's been swimming naked.
- It's far better to buy a wonderful company at a fair price than a fair company at a wonderful price.
- Our favorite holding period is forever.
- Chains of habit are too light to be felt until they are too heavy to be broken.
- We simply attempt to be fearful when others are greedy and greedy when others are fearful.
- Price is what you pay. Value is what you get.

At the beginning of this chapter I used the well-known quote from the Oracle of Omaha: "Be fearful when others are greedy and greedy when others are fearful." Buffett is called the Oracle of Omaha because he's such a smart player of the market. If you're going to read any book on how he invests, have a look at *The Snowball: Warren Buffett and the Business of Life* by Alice Schroeder, which was on the *New York Times* bestseller list.

In 1990, Buffett's company, Berkshire Hathaway, was a $US7,100 stock — pretty good, eh? Well today it's, wait for it, a $US304,500 stock! Imagine if you'd got on board with Warren years ago!

WHAT BUFFETT LOOKS AT WHEN BUYING STOCKS

When I invest in a company, I put it through some of Warren Buffett's key rules for assessing an investment:

- Do I like the management?
- Do I understand the investment/company?
- Can I write down the reasons for buying a company at a specific price?
- I avoid gambling with stocks.
- I buy stocks of companies that people use their goods or services daily. (Buffett held stocks such as McDonald's, American Express, Coke and so on because that's what Americans wanted.)

The Guardian newspaper looked at how Buffett invested in what was called "inevitable brands" like Coke, which dominate their sector. Gillette was one of them and this is how *The Guardian's* Sean Farrell explained the investment in the shaving company.

"Buffett viewed Gillette as another inevitable brand whose dominance in shaving products was akin to Coca-Cola's in beverages," he wrote. "Berkshire Hathaway began buying shares in the late 1980s and became Gillette's biggest shareholder. Berkshire Hathaway made an estimated $4.4 billion paper profit when Procter & Gamble bought Gillette in 2005 and Buffett's company became P&G's biggest investor."

I recall Buffett saying that he liked investing in a product that maybe 3 billion men each morning had to use!

MY ALGORITHM FOR BUYING STOCKS

Algorithms are perceived by many to be some complicated method for say picking and investing stocks. However, an algorithm is just a complicated word for a formula or recipe for doing things. In its simplest form, a recipe for making a cake is an algorithm.

PETER SWITZER'S ALGORITHM FOR BUYING STOCKS

1. Only deal with companies with a quality history.	✓
2. Like the management.	✓
3. Like the industry and its potential.	✓
4. Be happy with 10% annual return over a decade but hope to do better.	✓
5. Look for stocks beaten up by the market for temporary reasons e.g. when BHP dropped to around $15 in 2016 because iron ore prices had plummeted, this proved to be a good time to buy. When iron ore prices picked up in 2017, the share price went to $29!	✓
6. Make a "buy" decision on holding for at least 3 years.	✓
7. See if the charts support the view. I like the charts of the share price to tell me that the bottom of a share price fall is over and a convincing uptrend has started.	✓
8. Let the market move up before jumping on board.	✓
9. Make sure the company isn't more than 5-10% of your portfolio.	✓
10. Learn about what Price/Earnings and Earnings per share numbers tell you about stocks but don't be totally influenced by their messages. (Paul explained these terms on page 103)	✓
11. Know your investment strategy and stick to it, e.g. I collect reliable dividend stocks in the core of my portfolio and allocate say 10% of my portfolio to stocks that could return big jumps in their share price but could also disappoint and might not pay a dividend.	✓

This algorithm is compatible with my investment strategy. As your strategy differs, so will your algorithm.

RULES FOR BUYING STOCKS

The US website TheStreet.com outlines its 5 rules for buying stocks. Let me list them for you. They were written by Jeff Reeves of Investor Place:

1. Buy what you know.
2. Buy stocks that great investors own.
3. Buy stocks for the future, not the past.
4. Buy stocks in companies with great leadership.
5. Buy stocks with a clear plan to sell.

Benjamin Graham is the legend of the stock market that other legends, such as Warren Buffet, quote. He once told us that:

> *"The intelligent investor is a realist who sells to optimists and buys from pessimists."*

And again:

> *"An investment operation is one which, upon thorough analysis, promises safety of principal and an adequate return."*

ONE FINAL WORD...

Like the racecourse, the stock market can be a dangerous place if you go there to punt or gamble. However, if you select quality businesses that have a good history of paying reliable dividends, it's called investing. Be an investor and you will always be on a winner, over time. Be a speculating punter and you might have some wins but history shows that most gamblers end up with the seat out of their pants!

MY 11 COMMANDMENTS OF SHARES

1. Always buy great companies that stand the test of time. Remember Anne Scheiber, who always bought quality companies. Her strict adherence to the law of process resulted in a $22 million windfall for Yeshiva University.

2. Embrace a policy of not buying junk companies and stick to this like glue. It can be tempting to speculate on low-priced stocks but investing in shares shouldn't be seen as gambling.

3. Buy great companies when crashes create silly prices

4. Remember the stock market, historically, returns around 10% a year over a decade. Never ever forget that you're playing for the long term.

5. Buying stocks inside an SMSF, which is taxed at 15%, can mean a 5-6% dividend grosses up to 7% plus.

6. Use an adviser who'll make you stick to a plan.

7. Look at buying solid dividend-paying stocks or Exchange Traded Funds (ETF) as a core strategy.

8. Learn from the professionals who won't let their losses go over 10% and put automatic sell orders in, if the stock price falls below what's called their stop price.

9. Remember the past is never a 100% accurate guide about future returns. That said, I like to invest with long-term winners i.e. stocks that have a good history of paying healthy dividends and a decent capital gain.

10. Consider taking a subscription to our investment newsletter called the *The Switzer Report*. Paul Rickard and I write about stocks every week and Paul has produced a model stock portfolio, which he reviews each month.

11. Don't get caught not taking a trial to the *The Switzer Report!*

THE ACCIDENTAL INVESTOR
ANDRE

"He announced that before Christmas he was going to buy an exchange traded fund."

Meet Andre, a talented individual who started at Switzer with a lot of knowledge about film, video and photography and an attitude of team work and positivity. Andre had been employed by a multinational company but was looking for a change. They say it takes a genius to spot talent and I

saw the talent in Andre from the get go – so read what you want into that!

We hired Andre on attitude and for that he got a big tick. As for knowledge about finance, much to his Dad's lament, there just wasn't much there – though he's the rule not the exception. His job was behind the camera not in front like me so we didn't see that as a problem.

At the interview, he did intimate that he had a willingness to learn, and that's exactly what he has done.

After filming our inaugural education class (we run investing education classes and events at Switzer), Andre announced that before Christmas he was going to buy an Exchange Traded Fund. (see page 78 for an explanation of ETFs)

This is a guy who had no idea what an ETF was until he started hanging out with us and a pile of camera gear and lights.

However, he had two characteristics that were always going to help him win.

The first was that he was aspirational. The second, he has a willingness to change, which of course, keeps him open to positive influences of a Switzer kind.

There's an old proverb with a modern take that goes like this: "Keep company with the wise and you will become wise. If you make friends with stupid people, you will be ruined."

Andre has not only hung out with us, working with us he's had the benefit of filming and listening to the likes of Gerry Harvey, Tim Gurner, Charlie Aitken, Shane Oliver, Geoff Wilson and countless successful investors and entrepreneurs and has been learning from some of the best.

And there's been a family payoff, with his admission that he and his Dad are now talking investments. I can't recall who first made this clever observation but it's so appropriate to the story of Andre. "A young man should have a hobby and collecting money is a real good one." It's great advice for young women too!

Few of us increase our wealth through luck. When you look at Rich Lists, few have achieved wealth from being a CEO of a public or private company, unless they were big owner/shareholders.

The Rich List in *The Australian* shows wealth comes from starting businesses, investing in property, IT and other assets, such as shares.

Andre has been paid to hang out with some of the best money collectors this country has seen. And he often hears me quote the famous line from the comedian Sophie Tucker, (the one that's on the cover of this book and that I use often throughout it) who once reflected on her life and said: "I've been rich. I've been poor. Rich is better."

08 BEATING DEBT AND USING IT TO GET RICH

"Debt is not a dirty word."

Peter Switzer
(with a little help from *"Ego is not a dirty word"*
by Skyhooks)

"A bank is a place that will lend you money if you can prove that you don't need it." Bob Hope, 1959.

Neither a lender nor a borrower be. Yeah, right!

In the old world of 1959, the above recommendation was far more appropriate for the times. But that was then — now is different. Sure, banks are still uncompromising and you often find this out after a long-run relationship with them. But they, and their rival lenders for that matter, will lend to you for the usual reasons — to finance housing and business ventures. However, now they are increasingly happy to lend for more unusual reasons, such as buying shares. And you don't have to be a son or daughter of a media mogul or captain of industry to do it. The ability to service or pay off the debt is the critical issue.

TAKING ON DEBT TO BECOME WEALTHY

Q. What is the positive appeal of borrowers looking for money to buy shares or property?

A. Actually, it's something negative – i.e. negative gearing.

Q. What's negative gearing?

A. I know it sounds like it's something that's wrong with the clutch or gear box in your car, but it's just money talk for something pretty simple. Imagine you borrow to buy a rental property. The borrowing is called gearing. Now if you rent it out and received $400 a month rent, but your monthly repayment on the loan for the property and other costs were $500, then you've borrowed for a negative result. Clearly, you're out of pocket by $100 a month. That's negative gearing in a nutshell. Keep reading...

Q. OK, that sounds simple but why would anyone do something that puts them one step closer to the poor house?

A. Well, they get to receive rent, which helps pay off the loan. And those houses, over time, increase in value. In money talk terms — this is capital gain. Capital gain is the increased value of a property or any asset that happens over time.

Q. But hang on, don't people find it difficult to meet the shortfall each month? In your example, the difference was only $100 a month or $25 a week. What if it was say $80 a week?

A. OK, the answer is simple — the tax system helps. But the full answer takes a bit of explaining so stay with me on this. Let's assume after taking on board the rental income received, and then deducting the expenses for holding the rental property, such as rates, water, insurance, real estate fees, repairs, etc. as well as the interest repayments, the total 'loss' over a year is $4,640.

Q. That's a big loss, how is it made sufferable?

A. Well, just as income is taxed when you earn it, the tax system allows you to get effective refunds on losses. If the borrower was on a 47% tax rate (for simplicity), then to work out the 'saving' you'd take that $4,640 loss and multiply it by the tax rate of 47%. This equals $2,180.80. Now, if you take this away from your loss of $4,640, you wind up with a loss of $2,459.20. A loss of $2,459.20 looks more manageable than the hefty $4,640.

THE NEWS GETS BETTER

Q. Don't you have to come up with $386 a month (that's the loss of $4,640 divided by 12 months) to meet loan repayments etc?

A. Yes, but as Demtel's Tim Shaw once promised: "But wait, there's more!" Believe it or not, the good old Tax Office lets you fill out a form, which is called the PAYG income tax withholding variation (ITWV) application (NAT 2036). This informs the ATO when your overall taxable income will be reduced by such things as a negatively-geared property. This means that your paymaster at work can actually adjust your weekly, fortnightly or monthly tax to effectively give you your tax refund linked to the property early. Effectively, you get your year-end tax refund in smaller amounts every payday. That's a big help with managing your cashflow.

"Investing is not a game where the person with the 160 IQ beats the person with a 130 IQ."

Warren Buffet, the Oracle of Omaha

Q. What's the monthly refund in our example?

A. That would be $2,180 divided by 12 months = $181.67. So, you'd actually get this in your pay packet to help make the rented property play happen. Sure, it's still a gamble but if you get a nice property boom and your property is in a sought-after area, then the negatively-geared, personal investment decision could wind up as a real beauty.

BEING TAXED MORE IS BETTER
Q. It seems too easy to be true. Is it really a no brainer?

A. No, there are issues to consider. For starters, if you're in a lower tax bracket, such as the 34.5% one (including the Medicare levy of 2%), then the tax refund payoff isn't as big. The loss of $4,640 times 34.5% gives a tax saving of $1,600.80. Clearly, this is not as good as the $2,180.80, which is the tax benefit when your tax rate is 47%. It proves this point: if ever you have a choice between being rich and poor, definitely take the rich option.

Q. So negative gearing isn't for all income groups?

A. It certainly is more advantageous for higher income earners in higher tax brackets. The higher income person on $120,000 a year, say buying the exact same one-bedroom apartment in Sydney's Darling Harbour, as someone on $35,000, is in a less risky position, thanks to tax.

MORE NEGATIVES ON NEGATIVE GEARING
Q. So what else should I know about negative gearing?

A. It works better in a period of inflation, as this tends to push up house prices and rents. This can give you a big capital gain benefit. Low inflation can undermine capital gains.

Q. Doesn't inflation push up interest rates?

A. Yes, and the monthly payments can go ballistic, which could ruin the equation between income received from the property and the costs or outgoings of paying for it. In the late 1980s, interest rates on property approached 18% and not long after, a recession followed. The interest rate trap encourages many borrowed property owners to fix their rate of interest. This helps to keep the money equation fairly constant, though rents can fall during a recession.

LOAN STRATEGIES
Q. Are there any other loan tricks?

A. Yep, some people take out fixed interest, interest-only loans. These are harder to get for household borrowers buying a house to live in, but investors can access them, especially if they try a mortgage broker.

Q. What about paying off the loan?

A. Some people don't care about this 'little' issue and as long as they continue to get good capital gain, it's not really a big issue.

Q. How come?

A. Well, let's say you buy a unit for $400,00 and borrow $300,000. In 10 years' time you might still owe $300,000 because you only paid interest and didn't reduce the capital borrowed. But the property could be worth $900,000 and along the way, you would have picked up tax benefits from being a landlord. The $600,000 worth of equity (ownership) you have in the property makes it easy for you to borrow again for other investments.

Q. But you'll have to pay off another property and couldn't that increase your risk of failure?

A. Yes, and the critical issue for anyone going into negatively-geared assets is to work out how you would service your debt if something went wrong.

Q. What if I felt better about killing off the principal of the loan?

A. Then you can go with a variable loan, as the tax system helps with interest rate rises. Or then again, you could use a cocktail loan, which is part-variable and part-fixed.

Q. What can go wrong?

A. You could lose your job. Or maybe the loan you borrowed at 4% goes to 7%. Then your tenant could run off owing three months' rent or the place could be left without a tenant for a month or more. Of course, the body corporate could be told that there are termites and the repair bill could take $8,000 off you. Preparing for the worst-case scenario is what the guys in big business call "effective risk management." You need to be a risk manager too! Remember the SWOT I asked you to do on 'you' back on page 17? Every time you think seriously about adding an asset to your portfolio, you should do a SWOT on that asset. What are its strengths, weaknesses, opportunities and threats? This is what professional wealth builders do. Most people don't get wealthy by accident or by taking too many uncalculated risks.

"Ultimately, nothing should be more important to investors than the ability to sleep soundly at night."

Seth Klarman

Q. Could a rising value property mean higher rents and the negatively-geared property becomes positively geared?

A. Yes, but so what? If your income from the property exceeds the costs of running it, you lose the losses you had when you were negatively gearing the property (and the tax advantages) but you're now living with profit instead of a loss. That's okay. In fact, it's good. It makes it very easy to borrow more to accumulate more property.

CAPITAL GAINS TAX

Q. OK, you've explained negative gearing. But isn't there a capital gains tax?

A. Yes, but those who 'punt' using negative gearing are gambling that the capital gain, even with the tax, will still bring a nice dividend. And if you buy in the right area and don't have to sell in a recession, it usually pays off.

Q. What rate is the capital gains tax?

A. It's at your top tax rate but there's a capital gains discount. If you hold the asset for a year or more, you can halve the gain and tax is paid only on the remaining 50% at your marginal tax rate.

Q. Do you pay capital gains tax annually?

A. No, you'd only pay capital gains tax when you sell the property and smarties often never sell. They simply use the rising value of their property to borrow to buy more property. And provided they borrow well and can make it through the rough times of being a landlord (periods of rising unemployment and disgusting, costly tenants), then a new property tycoon could be born out of negative gearing.

GOING INTO DEBT FOR SHARES

Just like property, you can borrow to buy shares and the tax system makes it easier to pull off.

Q. Why are people so keen to borrow to buy shares nowadays?

A. The low interest rate environment and the good returns in the stock market have encouraged ordinary investors to take on these debt plays. These money-making ploys are more risky, especially compared to term deposits. Low interest rates have encouraged people to be as adventurous and thrill seeking as *The Wolf of Wall Street!*

Q. Can you go to a bank and simply tell them that you want to borrow to buy shares?

A. Yes, that's right.

Q. Do you have to prove they are good shares?

A. Banks will have an approved list of shares and blue chip stocks would be preferred. You have to prove that you can service or pay back the loan.

Q. And the losses can be treated just like the example with a negatively-geared property?

A. Yes.

Q. So I calculate my losses and deduct it from my fortnightly income and get my tax adjusted?

A. That's right.

Q. What's the catch?

A. Well, you could have stricter limits placed on what you borrow compared to a house. Banks will lend more for a house.

TRADING PLACES ON THE MARGIN

Anyone who saw the 1984 Eddie Murphy movie *Trading Places* saw the bad guys go broke when their margin loans were called in. Margin loans give you leverage to buy more shares than you're able to buy with your cash.

Q. What exactly is margin lending?

A. Here a lender might lend you between 40% and 70% of the value of a parcel of shares and will hold the shares as security.

Q. More explanation, please.

A. You have $30,000 and want to buy $100,000 worth of shares. The margin lender spots you $70,000 to make it happen and hangs on to the parcel of shares.

Q. What determines how much they will lend?

A. It depends on the share and how its price gyrates and how often it's traded (its liquidity).

Q. Does it have to go into individual shares?

A. No, it could be used to punt on a managed fund or an exchange traded fund, as well.

Q. What is a managed fund?

A. These can be called unit trusts, mutual funds (in the US), investment funds, property trusts or even cash management trusts. Small investors have their savings pooled to give the fund the muscle to invest big time for better results than a single investor could expect. People buy units in the unit trust or fund with their prices found in newspapers or online. When the fund is doing well and making big profits, the value of the unit goes up. When they're on a losing streak, the price sinks, much the same way as a company's share price can perform. The Switzer Dividend Growth Fund (SWTZ) is an exchange traded fund and investors buy units at a price shown on the stock market. With this money, we buy the 30-40 dividend-paying stocks the fund likes. You make money when the unit price rises and via dividends, which can be paid quarterly, half-yearly or annually. SWTZ pays quarterly.

Q. What is an exchange traded fund?

A. I have talked about ETFs (see page 78) before but let me repeat myself to make the lesson more memorable. It's a fund traded on the stock exchange. Some can be passive, with no human decisions about what the fund buys when money comes in. If it's a fund based on the S&P/ASX 200 Index, if the Index rises 10% in a year your ETFs unit price goes up 10% (minus a small fee such as 0.2%). These ETFs can be called an Index Fund because they track an index on the stock market. In this example, when the ETF's management receives some money inflows, they buy the 200 stocks in the Index in proportion to the shares' weighting (or importance) in the Index. That means more of the money would go into buying CBA and BHP shares than say Domino's Pizza shares.

BACK TO THE MARGIN LOAN
Q. How do margin loans work?

A. Imagine you want to buy a group of shares worth $100,000 and the bank says it will lend you up to 70% or $70,000. The approved loan to share value ratio is 70%. But if the stock market dives and your share value slides from $100,000 to say $80,000, then the ratio is 70,000:80,000 or 7:8 which is 87.5%. You would have to kick in $14,000 to keep the ratio at 70%.

Q. Why not borrow to your limit to get the maximum return?

A. By having a buffer, it protects you in case the share price tanks. The bank won't be able to force you to make more repayments or sell shares (which is called a margin call).

Q. It seems risky, doesn't it?

A. Yes, but this is the worse-case scenario. You have to remember that gearing or borrowing to invest changes the risk equation. If you decide to jump into this fast lane (and many have and are not in the poor house), make sure you do your homework on the pros and cons, or talk to a financial adviser.

The upside is that you can access many more shares than you would ordinarily. But remember, when you use gearing, it can magnify your profits but also magnify your losses.

Q. Provided I don't go over the top with borrowing to invest, does time in the market guarantee good returns?

A. Remember nothing can be guaranteed, although history points to the answer "Yes". The 10-year time period tends to bring happy results for many investors, especially if their selected fund or shares do well. However, some assets — funds, shares, bonds, property trusts — can have shockers.

That's why I recommend diversification of the assets you invest in so when some are doing badly, others might be doing well.

GOTTA BE A STAYER

You know it would be nice to make a quick killing on the market or in real estate and become a card-carrying member of the high-flyers' club, but the reality is that most of us need to invest wisely for the long term. The 10-year wait-and-see on property and shares usually brings nice surprises.

Have a look at this chart — you know, my favourite chart!

INVESTMENT PERFORMANCE: 30 JUNE 1970 - 31 JULY 2009

Total returns for a $10,000 investment with no acquisition costs or taxes and all income reinvested

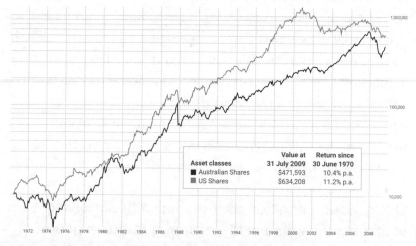

Asset classes	Value at 31 July 2009	Return since 30 June 1970
■ Australian Shares	$471,593	10.4% p.a.
■ US Shares	$634,208	11.2% p.a.

Source: Andex Charts Pty Ltd/ Vanguard Investments Australia Ltd.

The black line shows what happens to $10,000 between 1970 and 2009, which was one year after the stock market crashed by 50% during the GFC of 2008-09. That $10,000 became $471,593 but if you bought in late 2007 when that black line crashed 50%, you had a bad year. Your portfolio could have gone from $1 million to $500,000. But if you listened to me on TV and radio in early

2009 and invested in an ETF for the S&P/ASX 200 Index, you would be up over 130%, including capital gain and dividends! This chart makes me a long-term stocks believer.

This is a story that has been repeated over and over again. Sometimes around 10 years are needed for a big payoff. At other times, it's only five years. Sometimes, some other assets can do better than shares.

PROPERTY IS BETTER, SURELY?

In fact, the comparisons usually point to shares outperforming property but it does depend on what shares versus what property. Both are good assets and I love them both. As I've said before, history does show that shares over a 10-year period tend to return about 10% a year. But this is an average number. There could be two or three bad to ordinary years in the 10. However, there can be rip roaring years when the stock market index can go up between 30% and even 80% in a year! But remember, when all the bumps and booms are taken out, a good portfolio of shares should return around 10% per annum, of which 5% or half will come from dividend payments. That's why my Switzer Dividend Growth Fund specialises in finding good dividend payers. When you add in the franking credits, the return can be even better.

Q. What are franking credits?

A. Public companies pay tax on their profits at 30%. When they pay a dividend, they include what are called "franking credits", which represent the tax they've already paid. Shareholders can then apply the franking credits to reduce the tax they'd pay on the dividend. As I say elsewhere in the book, if you're a retiree or someone on a lower tax rate than 30%, you won't pay any tax on the dividend. Sometimes, you might end up with a cash refund as well. Franking credits can push a 5% dividend yield up to 7%. If you're on the 47% (45% plus 2% Medicare) rate, you'll pay tax on the dividend but at a much lower effective rate. Franking credits are a nice bonus for investing in dividend-paying stocks.

Q. Is this the full story?

A. No, I think the comparisons of stocks versus property have a few flaws. I'd suggest that everyone shouldn't universally plug for shares or managed funds over property but instead build up a wealth-building portfolio of assets, which includes both shares and property, along with term deposits and/or bonds.

WARNING

Q. What are bonds?

A. They can be government or corporate bonds and you can access these generally through bond funds, where a fund manager buys a collection of safe and slightly risky bonds to get, say, a return around 4-5%. If interest rates go higher, the returns can be higher. But as with all markets, there can be good and bad periods. But over time, they do well. Between 1970 and 2009, $10,000 in Australian bonds would have turned into $285,933 just after the crash. Bonds over a long time don't beat stocks but they do well.

> *"...build up a wealth-building portfolio of assets, which includes both shares and property, along with term deposits and/or bonds."*

We created the Switzer Bond Fund because we know investors trying to build wealth need diversified assets that are less volatile than shares.

MY OLD HOUSE

Back in 1979, my wife Maureen and I bought an old unrenovated place in Paddington in Sydney for around $50,000. When my father-in-law first came over and looked at it, his first words were: "Oh love, you'll have to try and get rid of this as quickly as possible!"

He didn't like its old age and he envisaged the endless weekends he knew he'd have to give up to help his egghead academic son-in-law restore the old Victorian cottage.

On his death bed, aged 88, he was heartened when he learnt we'd sold the house for $700,000. He knew we'd put about $100,000 worth of renovations into the house but also knew we'd brought up his two grandsons in the house/investment. It had reaped a great return.

Our Paddo house outperformed shares and balanced funds but we were lucky. Not all property matched Paddo's great rise. That's why the average Australian property returns don't often beat shares.

Certainly, if you understand real estate but don't understand shares, you could easily beat the stock market. However, for busy people who don't know property and can't watch the share market all the time, hitching your retirement play to a good funds manager, such as a super fund, which does the share picking for you, can be very rewarding in the long run.

09 INVESTING IN BRICKS & MORTAR

"Home is where one starts from."

T.S. Eliot (1888-1965)

I am not sure how money savvy T.S. Eliot was but he is spot on with this quote when I apply it to your investment strategy. I'm a believer in property and have told you that it's a key part of my portfolio.

If you're someone who's very suspicious of investing in shares, here's my property manifesto that outlines what you should know about trying to build your wealth by speculating on bricks and mortar. Of course, both shares and property are great ways to get richer but I understand why many normal people simply don't trust shares. However, I hope my earlier chapters talking about shares have changed a lot of people's views. For now, however, let's talk property.

STANDOUT STRATEGIES

There are two standout strategies to build your wealth. While both of these cash in on the nice parts of the tax system, there are a few fine details every investor should understand before laying their hard-earned income down.

The first strategy involves buying a home you live in, which can be improved and has lots of potential for capital gain. The second strategy is to buy investment properties, which also can and should bring capital gain. (There's a third strategy, which involves properties that might not bring great capital gain but still can be a nice wealth-building strategy. More on that later.)

KEEP THESE IN MIND

Before we look at the strategies, let's get a few property maxims (or rules of thumb) in your head:

- Buy the worst house in the best street.
- Buy where rents are solid and where tenants want to live.
- Research the price and rent history of the suburb.
- Buy the kind of property expected in the area.
- Remember sometimes the suburb next to a really popular suburb might have great potential.
- Buy the best books on property investment.

Don't forget these rules of thumb!

THE FIRST STRATEGY

Let's start with a favourite of mine: this is where you buy the worst house in the best street in a suburb that has real potential. If you see a trend in a suburb, with people moving in and renovating and house prices rising, that's a good sign the suburb has potential. You renovate wisely. Tastefully, but economically. You have room to expand and capital gain grows on your house. And the best thing is because it's your main place of residence, any gain you make if you sell it is tax free!

Over time, you can trade up. And eventually you'll have a great home that you live in until you retire. Along the way, you bank your leftover income into your home loan using an offset account and have a redraw facility in case you need the money.

This can be a tax-effective strategy. An offset account, could save tens of thousands of dollars off your total home loan repayments. What's an offset account?

An offset account is an account where you bank all your money. You put your wage in this account every week and draw out what you need to live from this account. Better still, you put everything you can on your credit card, first, take the benefit of the time you have before you have to pay, then pay the amount owing from your offset account. This way that money is left in your account earning interest that is offset against your home loan.

The beauty of this play is that you could easily end up with a home worth $2 million plus, which then could be sold and used to have a nice retirement. Some smarties actually have an investment property, which they rent out but eventually move into as their retirement abode. Capital gains tax will apply to this property, as it's a second home that's rented out. But if you live in this place until you die, then it will be your kids who'll have to pay the capital gains tax bill!

THE SECOND STRATEGY

The second strategy can be good for a young person who can't afford to buy a home or apartment where they want to live but could do so if they use the tax system by becoming a landlord. Imagine someone who really wanted a two-bedroom apartment at St Kilda in Melbourne (Victoria) for $650,000. They knew they couldn't make the repayment as an owner-occupier. But they could buy it as an investor and rent it out for five years. The rent contributes to the mortgage. In that time, their income would more than likely grow and/or they might get married, which not only brings love but also a second income. You, the one time landlord, could then move into the once rented home. Of course, there would be capital gains tax to pay if you ever sell it. If you owned it for 20 years, then five twentieths or a quarter would be hit by capital gains tax. However, there is a capital gains tax discount if you hold it for a year or more. This discount is 50%.

INVESTMENT PROPERTIES

Some people simply acquire investment properties and this is how they do it. The first place is bought for $500,000. They use interest-only money to reduce the repayments. The tax deductions also help. After five years, the apartment is worth $600,000 and the bank will give a loan on that $100,000 equity so the investor buys a second apartment for $400,000. The equity of $100,000 permits you to access a $400,000 loan. This is how many people build up a portfolio of properties.

Each time, your income has to support the repayments on a new loan but that equity in the first home helps you access another loan. Some borrowers can get an interest-only loan and a fixed rate of interest as well. Also, as their income grows, they expand their portfolio of properties accordingly.

As long as the properties are in well sought-after areas, you don't lose your job or a great recession doesn't come along, then you can apply this get-wealthy strategy really effectively. But, be clear on this, it is a risky strategy.

HOW PEOPLE TAKE ADVANTAGE OF TAX BENEFITS TO BUILD A PROPERTY PORTFOLIO

Negative gearing makes it easier to own lots of properties but it comes with risks. As I explained in the last chapter, gearing means borrowing and when the money going out is more than the money coming in from a rental property, you have negative cash flow. Effectively, you have a negatively-geared property. If the reverse is the case, then you have a positively-geared property. To simply explain how negative gearing helps you own a property, assume you earn $100,000 and the tax you pay is $25,717. But if you lose $10,000 on a rental property, your income falls to $90,000 and the tax will be $21,517. That $4,200 tax saving helps you pay the interest and other costs of being a landlord.

THE THIRD STRATEGY

The third method is a variation on the one above. While the latter property purchase relies on negative gearing, this one relies on positive gearing.

Here you buy cheaper properties where the monthly repayments and other costs are less than the rent you collect. These properties generally are slow to rise in value but sometimes their prices can rise a lot faster than many experts predict.

These properties might not be in flash areas today but the rents compared to interest repayments on loans linked to a cheaper property can make the whole deal work for you.

I always remember a friend who bought what he called "penny dreadfuls" in suburbs such as Redfern in Sydney and Port Melbourne in Melbourne, which were once despised suburbs but now are popular and expensive!

A NEW AGE STRATEGY

Some smarties are using their 'grannies' to get into property or to accumulate properties. This is a combo of strategies two and three. Imagine you buy a house with a decent block of land. Let's then imagine that you use negative gearing and the tax benefits to make it work.

Imagine you put a granny flat in the rear of the property. Now you have double income! If this idea appeals to you make sure you get three quotes from builders and get council approval first. Income from such an addition can really bump up your total rent collected without a very big jump in your monthly repayments on your loan. Some lenders will lend you the money to buy the house and then build the granny flat, if the numbers work out. Also, you could actually decide to live in the granny flat, which will save you the rent you pay now. This could really help you access an investment loan.

TIP: BRING IN THE EXPERTS

 I work on the idea that good properties can rise pretty significantly each year over five to 10-year periods, just like good shares. Always be careful about over-capitalising on renovations, though, because they will reduce your gain. Keep in mind that you may want to sell this property and the more money you invest in renovations, the less you make in profit. Make sure you get an expert to work out all the deductions you can claim as a landlord. A quantity surveyor can be a real help here. Great accountants and better still quantity surveyors can stagger you with the deductions that they show you, which you can legally claim.

CHECK *BEFORE* YOU BUY

Brad Porteus writing on realestate.com.au showed us what we should be checking before we dive deep into property.

1. Are there any water stains or corrosion on walls backing on to showers or baths?

Look for any signs of moisture penetration or water leaks. This is not a structural defect but can be a costly maintenance item for repair.

2. Check ceilings aren't sagging

Check ceilings to see if they're fixed flush into place and don't have a 'parachute' appearance. Shine a torch across the ceilings, as this will show up all deflections and defects in the ceiling sheets.

3. Check inside the cabinets in all wet areas

Is there a smell of damp, mould and mildew? These can be an indication of water leaks or even rising damp.

4. Check internal and external walls for large cracks

Visually check walls to note any large cracks. Cracks greater than 2mm in width or excessive cracking, can be a concern and should be further inspected by a qualified building inspector.

5. Is there evidence of mould in bath/bed rooms?

Mould can just look like dirty clouds on the walls and ceilings, especially if they have been recently cleaned. Mould has to be cleaned by professional mould remediation companies and can be quite expensive to have removed.

6. Check internal wall plastering for fine cracks

Check for fine hairline cracks (map cracking, as they take on the appearance of a map). These cracks are caused by the incorrect application of the wall plastering at the time of construction. Once these cracks are found in one area of the property, you'll usually find it in multiple areas.

7. Check the external roof lines

Look up the lines of the roof externally if possible to check if they're straight and free from deflections.

8. Check roof gutters aren't rusted on their inside

Check gutters from their top side to see if they're corroded and require replacement.

9. Do roof downpipes run to storm water drains?

Walk around the external perimeter of the home to check all roof downpipes are discharging into stormwater soak wells and not just on the ground. Look for any signs of past flooding or excess water flow around the roof downpipe bases, as this can be an indication that the soak wells are not suitably sized or require cleaning out, which can be a costly maintenance item.

10. Are drain holes on external perimeter walls?

This item is important for multi-storey properties. There should be small holes evident above and below window and door frames and along the suspended slab levels. The holes will usually be spaced approximately 1200mm apart. These holes allow water to escape from the cavity walls. Without these holes water can penetrate the internal walls of the home and cause ongoing and expensive maintenance.

BUYING A HOUSE CHECKLIST

There's a huge number of things to consider when buying a house. Most of them are more important than paint colours. With that in mind, Canstar has put together a 'buying a house checklist' — with a few (unemotional) things to keep in mind when attending the many houses you'll look at as a prospective home-buyer.

In short, consider the following things:

- Consider where you really want to live.
- Is the house close to important facilities?
- Does the house have enough rooms to suit your needs?
- Are the building and roof structurally sound?
- What are neighbourhood noise levels like?
- Does the house have good natural light?
- Does the house have adequate power?
- Is there any sign of termite activity?
- Are there any planned developments nearby?
- Is the garden suitable?
- Does the property provide sufficient parking space?
- Is the property at risk of flooding?
- What will some of the ongoing costs be?
- Where are the official property boundaries?
- Will you need to do any renovations?

Buying a property is such a massive investment for most people. Don't rush into any purchase —there will always be another property out there for you. And remember, do that SWOT that I explain on page 17.

BECOMING A LANDLORD OR PROPERTY INVESTOR

THE POSITIVES

1. The tenant gives you income

Use the rent to repay the loan you took out to buy the property.

2. Expenses are tax deductible

In effect, you're now in business. Having an investment property allows you to take advantage of a number of tax deductions.

3. Property gains value

Property prices tend to keep rising with inflation and often well beyond that. If you bought your property in the right area, you stand a good chance of reaping handsome rewards when the market rises. As property values rise, so do rents. If you decide to sell and you time your sale correctly, you can profit nicely.

"Having an investment property allows you to take advantage of a number of tax deductions..."

THE NEGATIVES

1. The tenants from hell

WARNING

Some landlords have all the luck and are able to attract long-term tenants who look after the property as if it was their own. Terrific tenants like this are worth keeping and rewarding with minimal rent rises. But you don't find the tenant from heaven every day. Quite often they come from the other place and are a pain to any landlord.

2. An oversupply of rental properties

 When there's a glut of rental properties on the market, it's called oversupply. This is when the law of supply and demand kicks in to the tenant's advantage. In a situation like this, property investors may have to take certain measures in order to attract tenants, ranging from asking for a lower rent than the market average to offering special deals, like waiving the first month's rent. The worst-case scenario is when you can't attract any tenants at all, and you still have to make payments on the loan you took out.

3. Regular maintenance costs

 Some property investors overlook the fact that owning a property incurs upkeep and repair costs similar to those for their own home. These costs can mount up and money needs to be set aside for them.

SMART BUYING

When all's said and done, the trick is to buy properties in areas where values are likely to rise faster than elsewhere. Keep your eye on the ball — continually educate yourself about property investment by reading books like this one.

The rules for buying an investment property are similar to the rules that you need to follow when buying your own home. However, an investment property has a few extra rules because the aim is to make money. Buying an investment property doesn't usually generate the same emotion as buying your own home does.

"...continually educate yourself about property investment by reading books like this one."

TIME FOR LEGENDARY ADVICE

In this book, I have continually encouraged you to do your own homework and/or go to experts to show you stuff that will help you make or save money to grow your riches. I'm going to share some great property insights from some of the best in the business of real estate.

My first is someone I've nicknamed the 'Princess of Property' — Margaret Lomas of Destiny Financial. Margaret has a business helping people invest wisely in property. Along the way she has won Telstra Small Business awards and has been a regular contributor to my radio and TV shows, as well as my websites.

I've talked about learning from legends and Margaret Lomas is a legend!

I asked Margaret to share with you some really important insights about getting rich through property. And she wanted to pinpoint some mistaken beliefs than can be costly to a novice investor.

6 PROPERTY INVESTING MYTHS

by Margaret Lomas

Listening to the property experts, you'd never guess it was the 21st century! They all seem to be teaching the same old strategies for property investing, and it's almost like we have never had any major change to our financial system, tax system and bank borrowing rules!

With the property landscape changing all the time, largely as a result of economic influences, savvy investors have to keep up, and realise that everything is changing, rapidly!

Here are my 6 property investing myths. Follow these religiously to ensure you invest effectively!

1. Blue chip properties in city CBDs grow best

I can't believe people are still clinging to this! Those who insist that only Central Business District (CBD) properties qualify as blue chip property, and only blue chip property grows well, clearly do little real research and are overlooking the significant evidence that shows that it is not the location in relation to the nearest city that impacts on how well a property grows. There is an abundance of factors that actually play a vital role in whether an area, and so an individual property, will grow well or not, and these factors make up the very important growth drivers of property. They include characteristics such as diversity of employment, access to health services, the degree to which median household income is growing, whether population growth is outstripping the national average, and access to lifestyle services. All these characteristics can be found in many areas, not just those close to cities.

2. The regions have good cash flow but lower growth

While the regions definitely do often show a better rental yield (the percentage return), most probably due to the lower buy-in prices and the relatively higher rent returns, it doesn't follow that they also always perform less well in terms of their capacity to grow in value .

In his *Iconomics Report*, Terry Ryder prepared a study covering the prior 15 years, examining property growth. This study proved empirically that many regional areas had experienced exceptional growth for the period, and that many CBD and coastal properties showed the most lacklustre growth of all.

While it's true that 'location, location, location' may be the key to good growth, it's not true that there is any link between that premise and the location being the seaside or the city.

3. You have to buy median-priced property, or greater, to do well

When an area grows well, it's usually the result of 'intrinsic' growth drivers. Intrinsic growth drivers are those qualities of an area that exist *within* an area – factors that are sustainable and ongoing, such as population growth, infrastructure planning and economic vibrancy.

When an area exhibits an abundance of such drivers, all property in that area will grow well, regardless of whether it is low priced or median priced. Having said that, the higher the price, the less well the property may grow because, as prices increase, less people are able to afford to buy property with higher price tags, and more people fall into those lower price brackets. Usually, this places more pressure on lower-priced properties, and I have found that, as long as the area as a whole is growing, lower-priced properties will achieve the best growth rates of all properties in that area.

4. You must choose between cash flow and growth

I consider that the whole point of buying property as an investment is to see an increase in the value of the asset, and the greatest possible income from that asset during the time that the investor owns it. The 'experts' have created this misconception that you must choose by continuing to validate the theory that a property can only have one of these characteristics, either cash flow or growth.

This is simply not true. Buying property, which has both, is highly possible. Such property always exists somewhere, regardless of the present state of the economy.

As an investor, your goal must be to ensure that each property you purchase provides the best possible growth, for the best possible rental yield during the period you own it. You want your purchase to have its best performance – its greatest period of growth and most attractive rental yield – just after you buy it.

5. Market timing is the key

You'll often hear property experts and those trying to sell an investment property tell you that "It's not market timing, it's time in the market".

My theory is that this is often said to help you deal with any short-term negative performance that the property they sell experiences! When someone is giving you property investment advice based around a single area in which they may have available stock, the likelihood that *that* exact area is the best available investment *at that moment in time*, and is the closest possible match to your own individual investing needs, is pretty unlikely.

It's true that if you keep any property long enough (with very few exceptions), the sheer time that you remain in the market will most likely smooth out short-term negative growth and cash flow losses, and the property will ultimately be worth more than you paid for it. Whether its future value is high enough to have made the overall performance strong or not is another thing, and often once you consider the holding costs, the overall returns can be dismal indeed.

However, if you want to build the best possible property portfolio that you can, one that outperforms the average, and contains properties that consistently deliver high returns, giving the greatest possible growth during the time you hold it, market timing is the key. You want to find an area on the verge of its boom, and have that boom occur during your period of ownership, and you want this to occur with every property you buy.

6. You must personally know the area you buy in

You should never fall into the trap of believing that you should only buy in the area where you live because it's an area that you know well. When people insist to me that they must at least start by buying in their own area because they know it so well, I ask a range of questions about their area. In virtually every case, I discover that the person in fact has very little knowledge about the most common growth drivers in their area, and what they actually 'know' relates to lifestyle features.

What you know about your area is all the information, which is relevant to you as an owner occupier. While this also becomes important for a renter – your potential future income-producer – this information is by no means the catalyst by which an area will achieve that 'better than average' growth. The information, that's crucial when you're looking to invest in an area, is data that local residents are unlikely to know about their own area.

As well as this, it's also unlikely that you will be lucky enough to be living in the area which, at the very moment you are about to invest, is among the top hotspots of the country. While I have seen it happen, more often an investor, particularly one using home equity to leverage into an investment portfolio, will live in an area that is coming *out* of its major boom phase. They have most probably been able to grow equity in their own home because their area grew really well, but by the time they decide to use this equity, the area has settled into its stabilised growth phase and it will begin growing *less* well than other potential areas.

Always remember that you don't have to live in an area to know it well. By the time I buy in any area, I can guarantee that I 'know' it better than the locals do. What I know about that area, though, relates to economics, and what the locals know is more likely to relate to lifestyle. Lifestyle features rarely create boom towns, whereas economic vibrancy is the cornerstone of a future hotspot.

TIP

Invest as if you live in the 21st century and you will achieve great things. There are many areas that are presently being ignored that will provide great yields and growth to those who buy there. These areas are easy to pick, as long as you understand what drives growth and the relationship between a growing area and its economic vibrancy. Things are more complicated than they used to be, but the market is no harder to pick today than it has ever been. (If you found this information useful, Margaret's website is: www.destiny.com.au)

BUYING YOUR FIRST INVESTMENT PROPERTY
By John McGrath

A survey a few years back by Mortgage Choice found that 43% of Gen Ys are intending to buy an investment property ahead of their first home. They're willing to sacrifice the First Home Owners Grant and stamp duty concessions because they'd rather stay renting where they want to live and suit their lifestyle and buy an investment somewhere affordable.

So let's take a look at my top tips, mistakes and traps for first-time investors. But first, here's the overall picture.

I think the key to having a great property investment is outperforming the market in capital growth. Yield is important but the serious windfall comes if you find an area with great growth prospects. This can be achieved by solid research, observation and calculated risk.

Imagine if you'd bought a couple of Paddington terraces in Sydney in the 1970s and held them until today. Yet Paddington then only had potential. Very few 'astute buyers' wanted to touch the area. So look around and try to unearth the next Paddington. Generally, properties within a 10km radius of a major CBD or close to city beaches (also within 10 to 15km of the CBD) will yield the greatest growth. Try to find the areas that are relatively unwanted and have the signs for future growth. In addition to location, look for areas that have access to cultural and recreational facilities (universities, art galleries, historical precincts, grand period homes, etc.) as well as a growing village environment.

And when all the research and box ticking is done, go with your gut instinct and be prepared to take a calculated risk.

> *"...go with your gut instinct and be prepared to take a calculated risk."*

JOHN'S 8 TIPS

1. Know exactly how much you can afford and build in a buffer. Get your finance organised before you look and factor in that interest rates might creep a bit higher. Assume a few extra costs in the first few years. If you plan for a few things to go wrong, you'll be okay if they do.

2. Focus on capital growth above all else. You will make far more money out of a great capital growth investment than you will out of one that has slightly more rental return. Of course, yield can't be ignored as you're generally relying on it to fund the loan. The highest yielding properties are those in greatest demand. I recommend two-bedroom properties located within one kilometre of a train station.

3. Register your details on the top real estate websites. You'll get first notification of new listings and some agencies offer registered buyers the opportunity to inspect new properties

before they are made publicly available.

4. Buy something that feels good. Many people say don't buy an investment emotionally but I disagree. If it feels great to you, then it will feel great to others if you decide to sell it.

5. Inspect at least 10 properties before you buy. Even if the first one seems perfect, make sure you see enough to really know the market and recognise a good buy.

6. Change the time you inspect properties. Open inspections are great for you to go back and see the property you like at different times of the day and on different days to make sure it presents well at other times.

7. Buy older style houses or apartments for better growth.

8. Take a seven-year view, as most property cycles revolve every seven years so make sure you can stay the distance to get real growth.

3 MAIN MISTAKES

1. Overpaying because you haven't done enough research. Much of your profit can come in the buying if you do it right.

2. Not putting in the effort required. Make looking for your investment property a second job, as it will pay more than your first job if you get it right!

3. Buying without emotion – real growth comes when you unearth a hidden gem so buy something that excites you.

HERE ARE 3 TRAPS

- Buying brand new. It often looks and feels great but capital growth can be delayed when you buy into a brand new building. Older properties often have better growth in the first five years.

- Over-extending yourself. If you can hold a property in a good location for seven to eight years, you should be able to realise a substantial profit every time. If you stretch yourself too far and have to sell, you may end up losing money. Make sure you can afford what you're investing in.
- Buying with friends. Although it can seem easier to buy the property you want if you go halves with a friend, it can come undone if you have different views or circumstances down the track if the time comes to sell. If you are forced to sell prematurely or at the wrong time, you may lose much of your gain.

"Make looking for your investment property a second job, as it will pay more than your first job if you get it right."

TIPS FOR BUYING OFF THE PLAN
By Steven Chen

Purchasing property off-the-plan can provide significant financial and lifestyle benefits.

From a practical perspective, buying off-the-plan allows prospective owners to plan and have sufficient time to ensure they have their finances in place, sell an existing asset prior to completion and secure the optimum loan to suit their circumstances. For investors, an advantage of buying off-the-plan is the ability to have an early pre-selection of the project. Off-the-plan purchases only require a 10% deposit with no progress or top-off payments until settlement, which is often between 18 months and three years. This means that a buyer is able to pay at today's price, and if the market is rising, they can achieve capital gain with an initial 10% outlay.

If purchasing for investment purposes, buyers can also benefit from depreciation for items including fixtures and fittings.

For the owner-occupier, there are also advantages with regards to lifestyle and surrounds of the property to suit their requirements. With off-the-plan purchases, in some instances, a buyer has the ability to customise floorplans and finishes to best suit their own individual requirements. Buyers also have the opportunity to select from a range of dwelling types and essentially choose their preferred layout, positioning and colour scheme.

While there are many advantages to buying off-the-plan, it is imperative that buyers have a solid understanding of what's required to minimise any potential risk. As with any significant purchase, it's important to thoroughly research the market, current values, potential for growth, and lifestyle benefits of the immediate and surrounding areas.

 Buyers should carefully look into the area for future development as the apartment you may consider purchasing could have its views or natural light reduced, or even eliminated. Future development may also impact your property's re-sale value both in a negative and positive manner.

 Another important task to safeguard your purchase is to research the developer and their prior development experience. It is also important to ascertain who the builder is and what projects they have previously completed to gain an understanding of the quality of workmanship and ability to deliver the project.

Spend time examining the floor plan to better understand the scale of the residence. Check the ceiling height and dimensions of bulkhead areas, which typically conceal air conditioning units and utilities, as these can have an effect on the overall aesthetics.

Furthermore, engage a lawyer who has experience in off-plan contracts and providing the relevant information to safeguard your purchase decision. Experts say: "Buying off the plan is risky so make sure you do your homework!"

> *"It is imperative that buyers have a solid understanding of what's required to minimise any potential risk."*

FINAL BUYER'S TIP: HAVE A PPP

Buying a property is one of the biggest deals of your life so approach it professionally, draw up a property purchasing plan (PPP) which sets out:

1. What you want to do
2. Where you want to buy
3. How much you will pay
4. How you are going to do it — loans, etc.
5. What expert help is needed
6. What your cash position will be after you execute your plan.
7. And what happens if interest rates rise? Could you cope with a 2-3% rise in rates?

Remember: No one plans to fail but many fail to plan and it often explains money disasters and cash crises in our lives.

> *"Watch Selling Houses Australia — it shows you how to make money out of property plays."*

Peter Switzer

TIPS FOR SELLING A PROPERTY

1. Spring clean is a must

Remove clutter and dust everywhere. If you can't do it yourself, hire a cleaner.

2. Floors, windows and mirrors

Should shine and twinkle.

3. Have the right amount of furniture

Keep rooms spacious so remove excess furniture. If your home is too minimalist, hire furniture so the place seems cosy.

4. Finishing touches excite the senses!

Ensure towels and manchester are clean and neat. And bring a little spring inside. Arrange vases of flowers strategically in every room. Bake some bread and brew some coffee before show-time for the house — excite the buyers' senses.

5. Don't forget to clean the outside

Mow lawns, rake leaves, trim bushes and remove cobwebs.

6. Snap a pretty picture

Take quality and powerful photographs, using a wide-angle lens. Shoot external shots in the daytime and evening. Wet tiles and driveways before taking the shot for maximum effect.

7. Remove pets

Nothing says 'no deal' quite like a slobbering dog. Air your house out a couple of days in advance and use air fresheners to give your property a fresh scent.

WHY I SUPPORT USING A MORTGAGE BROKER

When it comes to mortgage brokers, I always used a broker before I started my loan business. They'd get me loans cheaper than I could from a bank, and with much better service. The broker I used always came to my home or office at a time to suit me, not him/her.

A mortgage broker can do the legwork for tricky loans when normal lenders say "No" and can suggest you can refinance your loan at a lower rate.

You don't pay a broker yourself. They're paid by the lender. They generally receive an upfront fee and then a trail for the life of your loan. Does anyone really care if a broker receives a fee/trail from a lender if they're able to take a borrower from a 5% bank loan to a 3.89% loan?

Undoubtedly, some brokers in the past did wrong things and they should undergo serious investigation and possible deregistration. But anyone who thinks that Aussies will pay brokers upfront fees needs their head read. First homebuyers usually can't afford to pay fees and most of us simply don't want to pay. Aussies aren't great at paying upfront fees for advice.

If I have a million dollar loan and a broker takes my interest rate down from 5% to 4%, he/she saves me $10,000 a year on an interest-only loan. If the broker gets $1,500 or .15% trail, I don't care.

If you do consider using a mortgage broker, make sure they're part of a professional association e.g. The Finance Brokers Association of Australia (FBAA). See www.fbaa.com.au

MY 11 COMMANDMENTS FOR BORROWING & PAYING OFF YOUR HOME LOAN

1. Have a good deposit. The bigger the better. When you have 20% deposit, the lender won't force you into Lenders Mortgage Insurance.

2. Get the lowest interest rate possible. Use comparison websites and mortgage brokers to help you.

3. If you've borrowed too much and couldn't stand too many interest rate rises, then perhaps fix your rate.

4. Pay off your loan as quickly as you can.

5. Keep monitoring the best deals for loans and don't be afraid to switch but go through the pros and cons.

6. Check the comparison interest rate. Some lenders offer really cheap rates but when you add in fees and other charges, you could be paying a higher rate.

7. Boost your savings via smarter spending and throw the accumulated funds against your mortgage.

8. Have a redraw facility. If you need to access money you've used to decrease the mortgage, you can access it.

9. See how the First Home Owners Grant can help you. Check out:www.canstar.com.au/home-loans/first-home-buyer-grants/. Also look at the First Home Super Saver scheme, which allows you to access your super to increase your deposit;www.ato.gov.au/Individuals/Super/Withdrawing-and-using-your-super/First-Home-Super-Saver-Scheme

10. Treat the buying and borrowing process as though it's a crucial step in getting richer. A home helps you borrow for other investments in shares, businesses and other money-making strategies.

11. Don't get caught ignoring these commandments!

When did you decide that you wanted to understand more about money?

It was around the time we were buying our first property, due to it being a big life change — for the first time we'd have a considerable amount of debt. This forced us to think about our spending habits

and lifestyle choices. A couple of years after we bought our first property we were beginning to think about our next move, for an investment property. This sparked interest and questions around what more could we be doing, and how could we be smarter with what we have. So we began looking for a financial adviser so that we could talk through some of these questions we had.

Were you always a good saver?

No, I wasn't actually. When focused on saving for a goal, I definitely was. However I wouldn't have said I was a great saver. I have become a much better saver due to the nature of having a mortgage, and knowing that a certain proportion of my salary is put directly on to the home loan. Part of this is becoming aware of spending and keeping a good budget spreadsheet and looking at simple ways you can increase your cashflow. I have definitely taught my partner better ways to save during our time together, and we have found it's about making it a habit.

When did you get the idea that you wanted to buy a property?

I had a little bit of money saved and wanted to invest it somehow. As we were planning a life together, I thought that investing in property would be the best use of the money. I wasn't keen on shares due to my husband being called up for a margin loan call during the GFC, as well as not having a great understanding of the share market. The Sydney property market seemed like a better investment. It would also be forced savings.

Has that been a good decision?

Initially, it seemed like the 'right thing to do' getting into the Sydney property market. However buying property has been one of the best decisions my husband and I ever made. We weren't as financially savvy back then but we have been learning a lot throughout the process of selling and buying more properties over the years. We were able to come out on top with our investments and have managed to increase our asset position in doing so.

What are your money goals? Do you and your husband Charlie have the same goals?

We both do a vision board focussing on what we'd like to achieve in the next year and also the next five years. There are definite overlaps between them. I think it's extremely important to communicate regularly with regards to your finances, as well as what you're trying to achieve individually and as a couple. (Continued next page).

What do you think of credit cards?

Up until recently. I didn't have a credit card for a few reasons - it affects the ability to borrow and we were looking to 'upsize' and buy a new place. Also about 10 years ago we got into a bit of credit card debt and ended up doing a transfer to pay it off in full. Now we are better at saving and managing our finances, it has benefits. The card is good for emergencies i.e. when travelling or it can be used purely to earn rewards and frequent flyer points.

Are you a spendthrift or do you think about what you buy?

Ha!!!! This is a tough question as I'd say that we both definitely like the 'finer things' in life, and definitely fall into the 'spend thrift' category. Over time, however, we have learnt how to really think about what we buy in terms of our food shop, household items, insurance, energy bills, telecommunications and how to be savvy. The budget spreadsheet has also helped us greatly, as we have recently extended ourselves to buy our latest investment.

You're raising children. What are your future wealth accumulation goals?

Ultimately, we'd like to have financial freedom. To be in a sound financial position in our later years would mean less stress on us, and also allow us to spend money the way we want. Having sources of passive income later in life is a huge part of what we want to achieve.

Who was your role model growing up with regards to money?

I think my grandparents taught me the most around the importance of saving. My father was also hugely affected by the stock market crash in the 1980s and overnight life became quite a lot harder. It was at this moment, when my mother had to return to work, I recognised the importance of keeping a career as a female, and having enough 'rainy day' money to ensure that no matter what life throws at us, we can be as prepared for it.

You work with a financial planner – what motivated you to make that decision?

Charlie and I are aware of the importance of being financially savvy and making our savings and super work hard for us. Being time poor and also not being experts in the field meant that we needed some help to grow our savings. Our financial adviser has helped alleviate the stress of having to worry about things like setting up the right insurance, how best to invest our super in the stock and property markets, and also organizing things around tax time. They have also helped us set up some savings accounts for our boys that we can slowly contribute to these and grow them overtime.

What else would you like to say?

I really believe that being savvy with your money and savings is something that can be learned. It is always helpful to talk to others about what they are doing, however you should always have an open mind. Everyone has a different life story and relationship with money, so it is always best to get as many different viewpoints as possible, reflect on these and ultimately reach your own conclusions on what's best for you and your family at any given time. We would definitely recommend seeking the help of a financial planner/adviser, as we lead busy lives and don't often have the time required to fully think about planning adequately for the future.

10 SHOW YOUR S-U-P-E-R
A LITTLE R-E-S-P-E-C-T

"When you start really respecting yourself, those you love and your money, the result is that you start having control over your money. What follows from that is control over your life."

Suze Orman, US Money Expert.

Be clear on this: your super is a gift. It forces you to save into a financial product that is taxed very softly. We should love it like we might love a house or a car as it could end up being more valuable than a property and will definitely be more valuable than a car.

According to many financial planners, superannuation is super. The statistics they point to argue that most of us need a slice of the super action. In fact, many argue we are under-supered. But why are most of the money smarties backing super?

Why super? There are 463 reasons why!

While there's a number of very good arguments to take out superannuation, the most compelling is the actual size of the age pension — $463 a week! If you think you can live happily on $463 a week, maybe you don't have to read on!

Q. What are the appeals of superannuation?

A. Firstly, it is taxed in a very compassionate way. Secondly, it is a 'no brainer' for people who don't have a brain for long-term investments. Thirdly, you can't get to it, under most circumstances, until you retire. Federal Governments — be they Coalition or Labor — are committed to reducing Australians' dependence on the age pension.

Q. Are there better alternatives like a home or a managed fund?

A. There could be but for most hard-working people, who can't keep a full-time eye on financial markets, superannuation has a good 'safe nest egg' feel for a comfortable retirement.

Q. Where does superannuation rank in the financial scheme of life?

A. This is not advice, as advice must be tailored to suit the circumstances of the respective investor, taking into account age, wealth, plans and income earning potential, IMPORTANT but I will tell you what I did and continue to do.

MY PERSONAL STRATEGY IN A NUTSHELL ...

I paid off the mortgage on my principal home as a high priority. As a back up, in case something goes wrong, I have superannuation. Next, I own investment properties in areas where I'm betting I'll get good capital gain. (This works if you're paying a lot of tax and property prices have been on the slide or have been subdued for some time.) Any spare funds I invest in managed funds and individual shares that I like because they have potential, and look under-priced.

Q. Can I invest in managed funds or shares via super?

A. Yes. You could start a self-managed super fund (SMSF). My self-managed superfund is one where I can select my own investments from shares to funds to term deposits to even art, etc. Some super funds that many employees are in, such as Australian Super, let you select shares within your super fund.

Q. How do we know what we get with super?

A. If it's a defined benefit fund, there'll be a set equation that will tell you what your benefit will be when you retire at various ages. Long-serving public servants and some big companies have employees who are still in such funds. Information on these is best sourced from the actual fund, as the rules can differ from fund to fund. Generally, they are good funds that offer inflation-indexed pensions for life! If you're in one, definitely stay in it, if you can.

Q. So with a defined benefit fund, you're certain to get what's promised?

A. Barring bankruptcy or some other calamity, what they promise is what you get. These are a super deal, giving you some certainty down the track. This is good for your financial planning.

Q. What are the super funds where the final payout figures to me are linked to the fund's performance relative to the market?

A. These are accumulation funds. In fact, all defined benefit funds are now closed to new members. Anyone reading this will more than likely be in a super fund in accumulation mode (you're building up your super) or in pension (you're taking money out of your super).

Q. Can you tell me what I should know about these accumulation funds?

A. There are lots of questions but the key one is: where is the money invested? The options range from very safe to more risky. If you're young, the experts say that the very safe ones could be a little too conservative but as you get on in years, safety is often preferred. And if you have been in a fund a long time and have 'laid' a good nest egg, you can easily take the safe option. Late starters usually have to take on risk before retirement to try to get the lump sum needed to be built up ahead of retirement.

Q. What is regarded as the conservative option?

A. Generally this means approximately 70% of your contributions going into fixed interest investments and the rest into shares. As you cut down on fixed interest and take on more shares, you increase the return, generally, but bump up the risk.

Q. What about compulsory super?

A. If you're an employee, your boss should be socking away 9.5% of your gross wage into super. This is about 5.5% less than the acceptable savings amount for a secure retirement. Some experts say you should save 15% of your income in super over 40 years to be really safe and happy in retirement. But as long as you own a home and would be happy to downsize some time in retirement, then the compulsory super or superannuation guarantee levy should be fine.

GETTING MONEY IN

Q. Do all employers have to put in for super?

A. Yes, with a couple of exceptions. Almost all workers should effectively be getting 9.5% put away each pay day.

Q. What employees are left out of super?

A. If you earn less than $450 a month, then you'll miss out. Also, if you're under 18, you need to work more than 30 hours in a week. Depending on how their contract is structured, contractors may also miss out.

Q. Is the 9.5% calculated on all my wages?

A. Some bosses are more generous than others but by the letter of the law, super only applies to ordinary time earnings. This means regular wages, including shift loadings, allowances and bonuses. But overtime doesn't count!

There's also a cap. If you earn more than approx. $221,000, your employer doesn't have to pay into super any money above that amount.

Q. How can I build up my super?

A. You can do this a number of ways: via salary sacrifice, making after tax contributions to your fund (you can put in your own money); other people's money (e.g. a parent could put money in for you) and the Government might help you!

Q. What's salary sacrifice?

A. This is probably one of the best ways to save that I know. It's a no-brainer if you have the cash flow, and you have room under the super cap of $25,000 a year.

Q. How does salary sacrifice work?

A. You ask your employer to contribute an additional amount into super, out of your pre-tax wages. Although it's then taxed when it hits the super fund at 15%, because it's a pre-tax contribution, you effectively get more into super than if you'd made the same contribution from your take-home (after tax) pay.

Here's an example. Suppose you earn $100,000. On your top dollars, you're paying tax at a rate of 39% (including the Medicare levy). If you take the top or last $10,000 you earn each year as wages, you will pay $3,900 in tax, leaving $6,100 to spend (or put into super as an after- tax contribution). But if instead you salary sacrifice this into super, the whole $10,000 will go to the super fund. The super fund will pay $1,500 in tax, and invest the remaining $8,500. All up, you'll be $2,400 better off! (That's $3,900 minus $1,500 = $2,400.)

Q. What are the downsides of salary sacrifice?

A. The only real downside is that you lock the money away in the super system and generally won't be able to access it until you turn 60, perhaps even later. Of course, it also reduces your take-home pay!

Q. Are there limits to salary sacrifice?

A. Because it's such a good deal, yes. The Government says that you can salary sacrifice up to your super cap, which is $25,000 each year. This cap also includes your employer's compulsory 9.5%. So you can salary sacrifice $25,000 less what your employer is contributing. If your boss puts $10,000 into super for you, you can throw $15,000 into your fund via salary sacrifice.

Q. Will all employers do salary sacrifice?

A. No, but they should. Ask your employer or the accounts department at your place of work if they'll do this for you.

Q. And if they don't, can I still access the benefit?

A. If you're eligible to make a super contribution, you can claim a tax deduction of up to $25,000 for personal super contributions. This is subject to the same cap that applies to the employer's compulsory 9.5% and salary sacrifice amounts. If your employer doesn't offer salary sacrifice and you have room under the cap, you can make a personal contribution to your fund and get a tax deduction — effectively putting you in the same position as if you'd accessed salary sacrifice.

Q. If I'm self-employed, can I put $25,000 into super for myself?

A. Yes, you can contribute this amount.

Q. What's the tax deduction?

A. It would be at your marginal tax rate, say 39% (the 37% rate plus Medicare Levy of 2%), minus the super tax rate of 15%. So the deduction would be 24%.

Q. Can I throw my own money in on top of the employer's contributions?

A. Yes. These already taxed contributions of yours are officially called non-deductible contributions (or non-concessional) contributions. The ones that have come from your employer from compulsory super or salary sacrifice, or personal contributions you claim a tax deduction for, are called deductible (or concessional) contributions.

Q. Why the different names for contributions?

A. Concessional contributions are taxed concessionally. When your employer puts in the compulsory 9.5%, the employer can claim a tax deduction at a rate of up to 30%. When those same contributions hit your super fund, the fund pays tax at a concessional rate of only 15%. If you draw this super money out before age 60, you'd pay 15% tax on these contributions.

On the other hand, non-concessional contributions come out of monies that have already been taxed. When withdrawn, there's never any tax to pay.

Q. Non-concessional contributions sound pretty good, are they?

A. Yes but not as good as salary sacrifice because you have been taxed on those dollars in your pay packet at a rate that's usually higher than 15%.

Q. Are there rules about who can make a contribution?

A. Yes, they're all aged-based. If you're under 65, there are no restrictions. You don't have to be working. In fact, you can be fully retired and make a non-concessional contribution. If you're aged between 65 and 74, then you can make a contribution (including salary sacrifice or personal contributions for which you claim a tax deduction), provided you meet the work test. If you're aged 75 or over, only the employer's compulsory 9.5% can go in — you can't make a non-concessional or salary sacrifice contribution. Yes it sounds ageist and it is!

Q. What's the work test?

A. You need to work 40 hours over any 30-day consecutive period (in any one year). This is like working full time for 1 full week, or 1 day per week part-time for 4 weeks. It needs to be genuine work (paid), but you only need to pass the test once in a financial year. If you're between 65 and 74, you must pass this test to make a personal super contribution, which is capped.

Q. Caps? What caps?

A. The concessional cap is $25,000 a year, while the non-concessional cap is $100,000. Under the "bring forward" rule, you can put in $300,000 of non-concessional contributions in one go, but you'll have to wait three

TECHNICAL

years before you can make another non-concessional contribution. Obviously, a couple could get $600,000 into super every three years, or in one go if they had a windfall!

Q. Who can access the bring-forward rule?

A. More aged-based rules! You must be under 65 (or have turned 65 in that financial year to access the "bring forward" rule), and not have accessed it in the previous three years. If you have, then the amount you'll be able to contribute will be reduced.

And there's one further complication. If your total super balance is more than $1.4 million and less than $1.5 million, the limit is $200,000. Between $1.5 million and $1.6 million, the limit is $100,000. Above $1.6 million, you can't make any further non-concessional contributions.

Q. What's your total super balance for this $1.6 million cap on your fund?

A. Your total super balance is the sum of all the monies you have in super – whether you have just the one super account, or multiple super accounts. It includes monies both in the "getting in and building up phase" (accumulation) and "getting out" phase (pension). The contribution caps is measured at the start of each financial year (in practice, the day before being June 30).

Q. What happens if I exceed my concessional cap?

A. If you exceed the concessional contributions cap, the ATO will issue you with an 'excess concessional contributions determination'. The excess will be counted as assessable income in your tax return (effectively, you'll pay tax on the excess at your marginal tax rate). There's also an administrative charge.

By the way, you can elect to withdraw from your fund up to 85% of the excess to help pay the tax bill. Who says the ATO doesn't have a heart?

Q. What happens if I exceed my non-concessional cap?

A. If you go over the cap, you can withdraw (without penalty) the excess non-concessional contributions and any associated investment earnings on those contributions. The earnings are then included in your income tax assessment and will be taxed at your marginal rate. If you don't withdraw the excess non-concessional contributions, the whole excess will be taxed at the highest marginal tax rate of 47%!

Q. Nice to know the penalties for exceeding the caps, but what if I can't put in enough money in one year? Is there any catch up?

A. Yes, there is a catch up for concessional contributions, provided your total super balance is under $500,000. Starting from 1 July 2018 (the 18/19 financial year), you can 'carry-forward' any unused amount of your concessional contributions cap on a rolling five-year basis. Potentially, if you hadn't made a contribution for four years because you're off work having a bub or on a long holiday, if you had the money you could make a contribution of up to $125,000 — that's $25,000 times five years — in the fifth year. Amounts carried forward that haven't been used after five years will expire.

The first year in which you can access unused concessional contributions is 2019–20 and this super booster idea applies to both women and men.

Q. You said the Government can help increase your super — how?

A. For starters, there's something called the co-contribution programme. Here the Federal Government will give you money for your super but you have to make a non-concessional (after-tax) contribution to your super fund. If you do that, they will throw some extra money in up to $500.

And it works for anyone earning less than $52,697 a year for the 2018/2019 year. If you earn $37,697 or less, the Federal Government will kick in 50 cents for every dollar you contribute to your super fund in after-tax dollars, up to a maximum of $500 a year. So if you put in $1,000, the Government will stump up $500. What you get reduces by 3.33 cents for every dollar you earn over $37,697, until it cuts out at $52,697.

There are 4 tests to get the money:

1. First, if you're over 65, you must be able to pass the work test. You also need to be under 71 years of age.

2. The second test is that you must earn 10% or more of your income from eligible employment, or 10% or more of your income from carrying on a business, or it can be a combination of both.

3. The third test is the income test, which says you have to earn less than $52,697 to get any co-contribution but to get the maximum amount you have to earn $37,697 or less. Then you'd have to put $1,000 into super for the $500 'gift'. For this

test, income is your assessable income for that financial year, plus any salary sacrifice contributions plus any fringe benefits.

4. Finally, if your super balance is $1.6 million or more, you can forget about the co-contribution assistance from the Government.

If you don't have the $1,000 as a low income worker, then maybe a spouse or parent — other people! — could kick in some dough.

Q. What other assistance is available to people who are on low incomes?

A. There's also the Low Income Super Tax Offset. What this means is that the Government effectively rebates to the super fund the contributions tax of 15% that applies to concessional contributions. Your income needs to be under $37,000, and the offset is capped at $500 (it's calculated as 15% of your concessional super contributions).

Q. Do I have to apply for this low income offset or does the Government automatically pay it to my super fund?

A. You won't need to do anything – the Government will automatically pay it to your super fund.

Q. Is there any help for partners making contributions to their spouse's super?

A. Yes, you can get a tax offset if you make a contribution to your spouse's or partner's super. The maximum offset is $540 and is available if you contribute $3,000 to their super and your spouse's income is under $37,000. It is called the Tax Offset for Spouse Contribution, and phases down to $0 if your partner's income exceeds $40,000. Income includes their assessable income plus any salary sacrifice contributions and any fringe benefits.

Q. Can a spouse help out even more with their partner's super?

A. Yes, by using a contributions' splitting strategy. Once a year you can instruct your fund to transfer to your spouse up to 85% of your concessional contributions made in that year. Here's an example from my old mate Noel Whitaker from the *SMH*: "Mike is 52 and earns $145,000 a year and is contributing $25,000 a year to superannuation, due to a combination of the compulsory employer superannuation and his own voluntary, sacrificed contributions.

"He already has more than $400,000 in superannuation but his wife Helen, who has a casual job, has very little. His contributions of $25,000 will still be liable for the 15% contributions tax, but he can ask his fund to put $21,250 of it into her superannuation account. If he keeps up this strategy until he is 67, Helen would end up with more than $620,000 in her own superannuation account if her fund earned 9% per annum."

GETTING MONEY OUT
Q. When can I get money out of my super?

A. You can access your super as soon as you turn 65 – no questions asked. But you can also get it earlier provided you meet a 'condition of release'.

Here's a summary of when you can get money out:

- When you reach preservation age (for most people age 60) and choose to access some of your super balance as a transition to retirement pension, while remaining employed on a full or part-time basis.

- When you permanently retire from the workforce on or after your preservation age. (See definition on the next page.)

- When you terminate an employment arrangement (i.e. change jobs) after turning age 60 (without necessarily retiring permanently).
- Reaching age 65 (whether you're retired or not).
- When you have been negatively affected (see the first question on the next page) before you reach your preservation age.

Q. What is preservation age?

A. This is the age you can access your super, provided you meet a condition of release. For most people, it's age 60. Some years ago, the Government decided to increase it from 55 to 60 years of age and phased in the introduction. This means that some people have lower preservation ages, depending on when they were born. The table on below shows you these dates and ages:

AGES WHEN YOU CAN ACCESS YOUR SUPER

Year you're born	Preservation Age
Before 1 July 1960	55
1 July 1960 – 30 June 1961	56
1 July 1961 – 30 June 1962	57
1 July 1962 – 30 June 1963	58
1 July 1963 – 30 June 1964	59
From 1 July 1964	60

Source: Australian Taxation Office

"You can retire early but you can only access your super if you've reached your preservation age."

Q. Can I get my super earlier under special circumstances?

A. Yes. There's a limited but defined list that includes:

- Severe financial hardship.
- Permanent incapacity.
- Diagnosis of a terminal medical condition.
- Compassionate grounds.
- If you change employers and your balance is under $200.

In most cases, you'll need to lodge a formal application to the Department of Human Services (Centrelink).

Q. How can I take my money out of super?

A. You can take a lump sum withdrawal or through the payment of a regular super pension.

Q. Do I pay tax if I take out my super as a lump sum?

A. Most people won't pay any tax when they take out their super as a lump sum. There are three situations where tax might apply. Firstly, if you're a member of an old style defined benefit fund, such as public servants or employees of government-owned entities (I mentioned defined benefit funds on page 177).

Secondly, if you're aged under 60 but older than your preservation age (see the table opposite).

Thirdly, if you're under your preservation age and are allowed to take the money out early.

Q. What are the components of a lump sum superannuation payout?

A. There are two components. Firstly, a 'tax-free component', which essentially represents the return of your non-concessional contributions. The second component is the 'taxable component', which represents the investment earnings on your super plus the return of your concessional contributions. It is further divided into a 'taxed element' and an 'untaxed element'. Most people don't have to worry about the 'untaxed element' as it only applies to former government employees or members of a defined benefit scheme, as mentioned above.

Q. Can I retire fully before 60 and draw on my super? And will I pay tax?

A. Yes, you can retire early. You can only access your super if you've reached your preservation age. You won't pay any tax on your 'tax free component' but you could pay tax on the 'taxable component'. The first $205,000 of the 'taxable element' will be tax free, then it will be taxed at 17% (15% plus 2% Medicare Levy).

Q. When can I get my super money tax free?

A. Provided you don't have an 'untaxed element', then at age 65 (whether retired or not), or if you're over 60 and fully retired.

Q. What is a super pension?

A. Instead of taking a lump sum withdrawal, you can take a regular pension that's paid from your super monies (otherwise known as a retirement income stream).

Q. Are there limits on how much money I can transfer to start a pension?

A. Yes, the Government has put in place a cap of $1.6 million. Known as the 'Transfer Balance Cap', this is a limit on the balance of your super monies that can be transferred to start a pension. It's a lifetime limit but the $1.6 million can grow higher if the superfund in pension mode invests successfully.

One of the great things about transferring monies to support the payment of a pension is that when those monies are invested, the earnings (such as interest and dividends) are taxed at the best rate of all. Zero percent!

Q. How do I start a super pension?

A. Firstly, you need to be eligible. You must have reached preservation age and then meet a condition of release. Turning 65 is one of the conditions of release. Then, contact your super fund to start a pension.

Q. How much pension do I need to take?

A. Most super pensions have no maximum withdrawal. You can take as much as you like. They do, however, have a minimum that you must take.

The minimum withdrawal is aged-based and is calculated as a percentage of your super account balance. Because the Government wants you to use up your super, the minimum withdrawal increases as you get older, and also with a bigger balance. The table over the page shows you these minimum withdrawals:

"In the long run, it's not just how much money you make that will determine your future prosperity. It's how much of that money you put to work by saving and investing it."

Peter Lynch, legendary US fund manager.

AGED-BASED MINIMAL WITHDRAWALS

Age	Minimum withdrawal %
Under 65	4%
65-74	5%
75-79	6%
80-84	7%
85-89	9%
90-94	11%
95 or older	14%

Source: Australian Taxation Office

So, if you're 66 and commence a pension with an account balance of $1 million, you must withdraw at least 5% ($50,000) as a pension in the first year.

Your age and account balance are measured at the start of each financial year (1 July). If you start a pension mid-year, the minimum withdrawal is pro-rated, except if it's the last month (June) when none is required.

Q. How much tax will I pay on my pension?

A. Super pensions are generally tax free. If you're over 60, you'll only pay tax on any 'untaxed element'. Only former government employees or recipients of a defined benefit pension payment need to worry about this.

If you're aged between your preservation age and age 60, there could be a little bit of tax to pay on any 'taxed element' and more on an 'untaxed element'. I've discussed this before and more than likely this doesn't apply to you.

Q. Can I stop a pension and take it out as a lump sum?

A. Yes, you can generally do this at any time. This is known as commutation.

Q. Can my pension account balance be impacted by movements in the share market?

A. If you're exposed to shares in your super fund in retirement, the answer is "yes". That's why many older retirees reduce their holdings of shares.

Q. Can I draw on my super and keep working under the age of 65?

A. Yes by using something called a Transition to Retirement Pension (TRIP). This is where you keep on working and draw some of your pension. There are tax benefits to this.

Q. Who can do this?

A. Anyone who has reached his or her preservation age.

Q. What else do I need to know about a Transition to Retirement Pension?

A. You must take out at least 4% of the balance each year as a pension, and you can't take any more than 10%. If you're under 60, there may be a bit of tax to pay on your pension. If you're 60 or over, it should be tax free.

"You can draw on your super and keep working under the age of 65 by using a Transition to Retirement Pension."

INVESTING YOUR SUPER
Q. What do I need to know about investing my super?

A. You need to know two important points. Firstly, who's managing it (usually the name of the fund) and which investment option you've selected.

You can choose to know a lot more, such as details of any insurance cover, its investment strategy and mix of assets, how it's performing, and how much it charges – but at least cover these two points above.

Q. What is a 'default' fund?

A. The 'default' fund is the fund your employer pays your super monies into if you don't otherwise instruct them. Most employees are by law allowed to choose or nominate their super fund. When you start a new job, your employer should ask you where you want your super contributions paid. If you don't advise your employer, your contributions will go into their 'default' fund.

Often the 'default' fund is connected to a particular industry or enterprise award e.g. employees who work in retail shops often have their super in REST, the Retail Employees Superannuation Trust; building and construction workers may be with CBUS.
The 'default' fund will usually have a default investment option known as a MySuper Account. These are lower fee accounts that have a single diversified investment strategy. Typically, they take a balanced/growth approach to investing, with 70% of assets in growth (e.g. shares and property) and 30% in defensive investments (e.g. cash and fixed interest).

Q. How do I know if the "balanced" or "growth" option is right?

A. Most funds offer several different investment options. They usually have a name such as High Growth, Growth, Balanced, Defensive or Conservative. Sometimes they're described according to what they invest in, such as Australian shares or cash.

There's no right or wrong answer about what to invest in. But to help make the decision, the things you should consider include your age, how many years until you plan to retire, what investments you may have outside super, how comfortable you are with risk i.e. the risk that your super could go backwards in the short term.

Typically, we break investment assets into two main categories: growth and income. Growth assets include Australian shares, overseas shares and property. A big part of the return should come from the asset going up in price. On the other hand, income assets, such as cash and fixed interest, should be relatively stable in value and almost all the return should come from the income they pay.

Growth assets are more risky but offer the prospect of higher returns. Income (or defensive) assets are typically less risky and offer lower, but usually more reliable, returns.

To get an idea about the mix of growth assets and income assets, the table over the page from ASIC's MoneySmart website shows a typical mix according to age. If you're young and won't retire for a long time, ideally you'll want to have most of your super in growth assets. A 'growth' or 'high growth' mix may suit. As you move into your fifties, you may want to tone the risk down a touch and have a 'balanced' strategy. As you approach retirement, you may want to move this back to a more 'capital stable' or 'conservative balanced' mix.

TYPICAL MIX FOR A LIFECYCLE INVESTMENT STRATEGY

Age	Growth	Defensive
Under 45	85%	15%
45-54	75%	25%
55-64	55%	45%
65 or older	40%	60%

Source: ASIC, MoneySmart

Q. Are there fees for super?
A. Yes, several, of course but they're on the way down.

There are 4 main types of fees:
1. Firstly, an administrative fee for the cost of looking after your account. In Industry Funds, this is typically $1.50 a week. In some older Retail Funds, this can be a lot higher.
2. Next, and probably the most important, the investment management fee. It depends on the type of fund, the type of investment mix and the manager. Charged on your total super assets, the range is 0.50% a year up to as high as 2.5%! Most Industry Funds are around 0.70% a year and Retail Funds are around 1.1% a year. Bottom line: if you're paying more than 1.25% a year, it's time to move – you're getting ripped off!
3. If you're drawing a pension, you'll probably be charged an

additional fee of around 0.10% a year.

4. Finally, there can be some miscellaneous fees, such as exit fees or a charge for splitting contributions.

Q. Do I need insurance in super?

A. No, you don't. In fact, if you're "foot loose and fancy free" and don't have any dependants or debt, you probably have rocks in your head if you take out insurance. You can "opt out".

But insurance in super will make sense for many people. By insurance, we mean life insurance, total and permanent disability (TPD) insurance and income protection.

You can take out insurance inside or outside of super. Generally, taking insurance inside super will be the cheapest and easiest option. This is because the super funds negotiate on scale and have group buying power, don't require medical check-ups and the premiums will often be tax deductible inside the fund (which lowers the cost). You can also pay for the insurance out of your pre-tax dollars (deducted from your super contributions).

If you take insurance outside super, you'll pay for it from "post-tax" dollars, and only the premium for income protection will be tax deductible. Of course, there are also downsides with inside super – "one size fits all", cover limits etc.

"...if you're foot loose and fancy free and don't have any dependants or debt, you probably have rocks in your head if you take out insurance."

THE QUESTION EVERYONE ASKS
Q. How much should I kick into super?
A. According to the industry, your super equation should come out with a final figure in retirement of 75% of your wage or salary.

Q. When is the best time for super?
A. If you start early, such as when you first start work, and throw in compound interest (i.e. the rolling over of interest on interest year after year), super should deliver a great retirement gift. In case you've left your run too late, you can bump up your super plays between 45 and 65 years of age and still get a good result.

Q. If I want 75% of my final salary each week when I retire, how much should I be putting into super now?
A. If you're 25, you should be putting in between 16-20%. At 35 years of age, try 24-30%. For those 45, it's in the 40-49% area and at 55 years of age, 89-108%.

Note, the lower figures are more appropriate for males, while females should look at the higher number in each range because statistically women live longer than men!

Q. Is there much more to know about super?
A. Yes, and the more you know, the better. However, if you don't have a retirement plan in place, time is running out, so get moving. That means reading, researching and ultimately, contributing. Killing debt and re-routing your funds into investments such as super represents a smarter use of your money. This is especially so if the person we're talking about is hard working and totally ill-prepared to be their own financial planner.

RUNNING YOUR SUPER
Q. Are there maximum amounts of money you can have in a super fund?

A. "No", but when you retire if you have over $1.6 million in your fund you'll be made to transfer the amount to an accumulation fund, where your earnings will be taxed at 15%. This is known as the Transfer Balance Cap – the maximum amount that you can transfer into the pension phase of super.

Q. So before I retire I could have $5 million in my super?

A. Yep, but getting that kind of money is very hard nowadays because there are contribution caps as I've said on page 183.

Q. If I work for myself, how do I access super?

A. If you own a company that you work for, then by law your company must put 9.5% of your gross pay into super because you're an employee of your own company. If you're a sole trader or partner, you simply select a super fund and put money in. You are governed by the same caps.

Q. What if my super fund after I retire grows over the $1.6 million limit?

A. The $1.6 million cap applies to how much money you can transfer into the pension phase and commence an income stream, such as an account-based pension. If the value of the underlying investments supporting the account-based pension then grows over $1.6 million, that's OK.

"...the maximum amount that you can transfer into the pension phase of your super is $1.6 million"

Q. How is tax different for retirees compared to those who work?

A. Retirees, who have met certain conditions, won't be taxed on earnings and on taking money out of super. Anyone not retired has earnings inside super taxed at 15% and will be taxed 15% or 30% on contributions, depending on their income.

Q. Who gets taxed 30% on contributions?

A. Most workers get taxed at 15% on their concessional contributions but high-income earners get taxed 30%. The threshold is $250,000 and it's tested on what's known as your income for surcharge purposes. Technically, the higher tax rate is also known as a Division 293 tax and it applies to all your concessional contributions.

Q. How do you define income for the higher contribution tax purposes?

A. This is the same as the calculation for the Medicare Levy Surcharge but excludes reportable super contributions. It includes your taxable income (assessable income minus allowable deductions), total reportable fringe benefits, any net financial investment loss or rental property loss and any net amount on which family trust distribution tax has been paid. If you don't understand this, worry about it when you start earning $250,000 a year!

Q. Does the super fund I belong to at work pay tax?

A. Yes, it pays 15% on earnings from its investments.

LUMP SUM TACTICS

Q. If I decide to take a lump sum instead of a super pension, how much do I need?

A. The experts say you'll need around 10 times your final salary to keep your life at a level to which you've become accustomed. So if you finish on $70,000, your lump sum should be a whopping $700,000!

Q. What should someone do if they're preparing to be a "lump sum type" in retirement.

A. Financial planners advise:

- Get rid of the mortgage, as this locks you into interest repayments that aren't tax deductible.
- The next trick is to opt for salary sacrifice, which could pump a large amount of dough into superannuation.

Now it's time to get geared up to buy shares and units in property trusts. Using professional advice, you get a tax smart portfolio plan constructed. Your savings are used to pay off the loan and you get tax deductions for the interest. Ultimately, if you want to live in the fast lane in retirement, you'll have to opt for the high-growth portfolios over balanced growth ones. For high returns, you shoulder more risk.

Q. What is the difference?

A. The higher growth funds have more shares and less cash and fixed interest investments, which are regarded as safer than shares.

"if you do take your super as a lump sum when you retire, it's best to get financial advice."

SUPER RICH SECTION

Q. Why should someone put their money into super?

A. It's tax effective. Historically, it has generated higher returns than term deposits. If you are bankrupted, the debt collectors generally can't touch your super but they can take your house!

Q. Are there better ages to be super-committed to super?

A. If you start early, you won't have a super problem. If you leave it late, don't procrastinate once you hit 50 years of age!

Q. How can I rate my super fund?

A. Go to chantwest.com.au or superratings.com.au to see the best funds in terms of returns over 3, 5, and 10 years. Then look up what they charge and then compare the best with your fund.

Q. What is the difference between a retail and industry super funds?

A. Retail funds are usually run by financial institutions, such as banks, while industry funds are run by trade unions and employer groups. Industry funds have a better performance record and generally are less expensive.

Q. How costly is it to ignore the costs of my super fund?

A. It can be very costly to ignore fees and charges. Over a long period (remember, you might be putting money into super for 30 or 40 years, and taking it out for another 30 or more years), an extra 1% each year in fees could reduce your retirement benefit by tens of thousands of dollars.

Q. How easy is it to transfer super funds? How do I do it?

A. Now, it's very easy. Contact the super fund you want to transfer to, and they will do the hard work!

Q. Is it costly to have more than one super fund?

A. Yes, why pay two sets of fees? The only good reason to have more than one super fund is if one of the funds has specific features, such as superior insurance cover (for example, specific occupation cover or higher cover), or allows you to invest in particular investment assets. Otherwise, just have one — and select the investment option that best meets your needs.

Q. If I have $2 million in my super fund — what should I do?

A. You've got to start retirement with a cap of $1.6 million. If you're at $2 million, you have to take $400,000 out. It can go into a super account in accumulation mode, where you'll pay 15% on its earnings. You could take out the $400,000 as a lump sum and invest it elsewhere or go on a long holiday! A very long holiday! Your partner, if they're under 65 or meet the work test, might also be able to put some of that $400,000 of your super into their super fund (see page 187 and the next answer).

Q. Can I give some super to my partner/wife/husband?

A. No, you can't 'give' your super away. But you can help your partner or spouse by "splitting" your contributions. You can split some or all of your concessional contributions (up to $25,000) so that they're effectively transferred to your spouse — building his or her super balance. You can do this after the end of the financial year by contacting your fund and completing the relevant ATO form. Your spouse must be under 65.

Q. Is it better to put extra money from windfalls into super or into paying off my home loan?

A. This depends a little bit on the interest rate and your "comfort factor", but most people will usually put the windfall into paying off their home loan. While you might be able to grow your wealth faster with super (if you were paying interest on your home loan at 5% a year from after tax dollars, you'd want your super fund to be earning at least 7% a year), the downside with super is that you won't be able to access the funds until you turn at least 60. Also, paying off your home loan "feels good" (note, if you have a redraw facility, you may want to keep a small balance outstanding).

Q. Is more money going into super better than going into an investment property?

A. This depends on what sort of property investor you are and your marginal tax rate. Remember, the interest on your investment property loan is going to be tax deductible. If you're good with property (know when and how to buy, how to manage and sell and can get the benefits of negative gearing), then look at property. Otherwise, put it into super. And you can have the best of both worlds by using an SMSF to buy an investment property, but you really need to know what you're doing with this strategy (see page 207).

Q. If I spend all my super, can I then go on the pension?

A. Yes, subject to passing the income and assets tests.

Q. What are these tests that you have to pass to get a full or part-pension and can you also receive a super pension?

A. As I said, there are two tests to pass – an assets test and an income test. Your home is not counted as part of the assets test, but most other assets (including your super) are. Potentially, you can receive a super pension and the government age pension.

If you're single and own your home, your total assets must be less than $258,500 to receive a full government pension. To get any part pension, they must be less than $567,250.

For a couple, the Government looks at your combined assets. A higher threshold applies for a couple who don't own their home. The table below sets out the asset thresholds.

PENSION ASSETS TEST THRESHOLDS*

	Access Full Pension	Access Part Pension
Single homeowner	$258,500	$567,250
Single non-homeowner	$465,500	$774,250
Couple homeowner	$387,500	$853,000
Couple non-homeowner	$594,500	$1,060,000

* Effective 20/3/19
Source: Australian Department of Human Services

There's also an income test to pass (higher threshold for couples). This gets a little more complicated because a "deemed" rate of earnings is applied to financial assets, including superannuation, shares, or term deposits.

The test (assets or income) that gives you the worst outcome (lowest pension) is the test that's applied!

Q. What do you mean by "deemed" rate of earnings?

A. In recent years there has been a growth in people wanting to make their own decisions when it comes to super. Running your own self managed super fund (SMSF) is easier said than done but the cost of running your fund can be cheaper and if you're prepared to spend time learning to invest like a professional, they can be more rewarding.

Q. How important is it to read my super statement carefully? And what should I be looking for?

A. As boring as it sounds, it is important to read this. Firstly, to check that all your contributions are going in. Next, to see what fees you're being charged, including any insurance premiums. Finally, to see what investment return you've earned.

Q. Is there any help for mums at home raising kids?

A. Yes, the super co-contribution (where the Government chucks in up to $500) and a tax offset that your partner gets (where he or she contributes up to $3,000 to your super) IMPORTANT can help. (See page 187)

Q. Do dads at home get help?

A. Yes, same as for mums.

After reading this chapter, I hope you're getting the idea that your super is a great asset and will assist you to have a comfortable retirement. I borrowed the words of the late, great Aretha Franklin when I called this chapter Show Your S-U-P-E-R a little R-E-S-P-E-C-T. Now let's spend some time talking about Do-It-Yourself (DIY) super or how to set up and run a self managed super fund (SMSF).

A SELF MANAGED SUPER FUND (SMSF)
Q. Why would I consider setting up a self managed super fund?

A. Running a self managed super fund (SMSF) isn't for everyone but it can be rewarding.

Here are 5 reasons for setting up an SMSF:

1. You want to control your investment strategy and investment selections.
2. You think you can invest and administer your super at a lower cost than that charged by retail or industry funds.
3. You run a small business and it owns property. You can get your SMSF to purchase the business property and lease it back to your business.
4. You want to use your super to invest in a residential investment property; or
5. You want your super to invest in more exotic assets, such as artwork, collectibles, commodities or currencies.

Q. Is there a minimum amount I need in super to make the switch from my current fund to an SMSF?

A. The more you have in your SMSF, the less the impact of fixed costs, such as audit fees, a supervisory levy to the ATO and accounting and/or administration costs. You need at least $200,000 to start and then aim to build that amount up as soon as you can. Remember, you can have to up to four members in your SMSF, and you can achieve this minimum $200,000 amount by summing the balance of all members.

Q. Is it difficult to run an SMSF?

A. No, but you either need to know what you're doing or pay for the right experts to help you, such as an accountant, administrator or financial adviser. Even if you access help, as a trustee, you're still ultimately responsible for what happens with the SMSF. Make sure you get a good handle on the obligations and rules before you decide to set up an SMSF.

Q. Is it costly to run an SMSF?

A. There are some costs that you can't avoid, such as an annual audit fee, a supervisory levy charged by the ATO and potentially ASIC and actuarial fees. You might also choose to have an accountant or professional administrator assist you and possibly a financial adviser to help with the investment strategy. And then if you're investing in managed products, there's also the indirect cost of the investment manager's fee. But depending on the size of the SMSF, you should be able to run it for less than 1%. Some big funds will get their annual costs down to 0.5% of their assets. Very few SMSFs incur costs under $3,000 each year.

Q. What are the main obligations with an SMSF?

A. The main obligation is to ensure that the fund is maintained for the purpose of providing benefits to its members on their retirement. This is known as the sole purpose test and is set down in law! Practically, this means investing the assets in accordance with the fund's investment strategy and relevant super laws, paying benefits and accepting

IMPORTANT

member contributions in accordance with the super laws, keeping proper books and records for up to seven years and having the accounts audited each year by an external auditor, submitting an annual return to the ATO and various other compliance obligations.

Q. Can you get someone else to do these obligatory tasks for you? An accountant? A financial adviser?

A. Yes, you can "outsource" these obligations. But you're still responsible for their actions.

Q. What assets can I invest in with an SMSF? Art? Stamps? Vintage cars? Wine?

A. Practically speaking, your SMSF can invest in almost any asset, provided it's in accordance with the fund's investment strategy. You and the other trustees are required by law to determine the investment strategy. But there are rules you need to follow around certain assets, such as collectibles (artwork, coins, stamps etc); you can't purchase some assets from related parties (your SMSF can't buy your holiday home); and related parties can't use the fund's assets for personal use (e.g. you can't rent out an investment property to your son/daughter). There are also limits on 'in-house assets', such as a family company. No more than 5% of the fund's total assets can be invested in 'in-house' assets.

Q. How do I go about buying a house with an SMSF?

A. Your SMSF can buy a residential investment property (but not from a related party). Your fund can finance this by borrowing through a special type of loan, which is technically known as a limited recourse borrowing arrangement (LRBA). Not all banks offer loans for these purposes and the maximum LVR (loan-to-valuation ratio) is generally 70%. These loans are more expensive than your typical home loan and there will be extra costs in setting up a bare trust to hold title to the property. Because the bank's only recourse is to the property itself (and not the other assets of your SMSF), you and the other trustees may be required to provide personal guarantees.

Borrowing to invest in property through your SMSF can be a good strategy if you understand the property market and can hold the property long enough (until you retire) so that you don't pay any capital gains tax on its sale.

Q. Can I buy a block of land in my SMSF?

A. Yes. You can also use borrowed money to buy a block of land. However, you can't use any of the borrowed money to improve it, say by building a house, nor can you use other monies in your SMSF to build the house. There's a whole set of rules around SMSF loans (limited recourse borrowing arrangements or LRBAs) that say that monies can't be spent on improvements, nor can you change the substantive nature of the asset.

Q. Can I borrow to buy a house and also for renovations?

A. No, you can't use borrowed monies to improve the asset. You can use other monies inside your SMSF to fund renovations, provided the property doesn't fundamentally become a different asset. A house can't become a block of flats but it can have another level added to it.

WARNING

Q. How much can I change the property?

A. It must meet the test of the "single acquirable asset" – it can't be fundamentally different or have a different purpose (i.e. change from residential to commercial).

Q. What are the conditions that go with buying a property inside an SMSF? Can I rent it to a family member?

A. Business properties are treated very differently to residential properties. If it's a residential property, your SMSF can't acquire it from a related party or rent it to a related party. The definition of a related party is broad and includes your spouse, children, parents, siblings, uncle, nephew and any of their controlled entities, such as a family trust or family company.

Q. Can my SMSF buy my factory from me? How would that work?

A. Yes, business premises are exempt from the related parties prohibition and aren't classified as 'in-house' assets. So your SMSF can buy your factory. The transaction must be on a commercial basis and you would need a valuation. I'd check with your accountant/financial adviser on this.

Q. Can I charge any rent?

A. Yes, your business can then rent the factory from your SMSF. Again, arrangements should be on an arm's length basis i.e. proper lease, market rent paid etc. Usually it's a good idea to get an opinion in writing (perhaps from a real estate agent) confirming the market rental.

Q.Can my super fund lend money to a family member?

A. No, the super laws expressly forbid lending money to a member or a relative of a member.

WARNING

Q. Can my business borrow from my super fund?

A. Yes, but subject to the 'in-house' assets test. This says that your SMSF can't have more than 5% of its total funds invested in 'in-house' assets, which includes loans to related parties, such as a business controlled by one of the members.

Q. How much would it cost?

A. You should charge a commercial rate of interest.

Q. Do I have to have insurance with an SMSF?

A. No, you don't have to take out insurance but the law requires that as part of the review of your SMSF's investment strategy, you should consider the insurance needs of the members.

Q. Is there any more you could learn about superannuation?

A. There sure is but what I've gone through with you in this chapter gives you more than the core of information you need to be on top of your super.

A FINAL NOTE

To test your respect of your money invested in super, go to the moneysmart.gov.au website and find out what your super fund will give you when you retire. It takes a couple of minutes but it will make you think about how you can grow your super via opting for more growth, by cutting your fees and finding a better performing fund. But you'll never ever know if you never ever go!

As I said at the beginning of this chapter, your super is a gift. It forces you to save into a financial product that's taxed very softly. Don't ignore your nest egg.

Good luck with building your super. Remember, it's a great asset, which could prove to be better than property but this will depend on being in a good performing fund and one that doesn't overcharge you for a hell of a long time!

MY 11 SUPER COMMANDMENTS

1. Respect your super. Know all the key rules. And always read your super statement!

2. Know exactly the super option you're in — growth, balanced or conservative — so you can tell people if you're asked.

3. Check out the tables that show you the best and cheapest super funds — your future wealth depends on this! Go to www.superratings.com.au.

4. Find out the costs that your super fund charges you (it's called your MER or marginal expense ratio). Try to get those costs down, while ensuring you're in a good performing fund. Failure to do so could cost you tens of thousands of dollars!

5. Don't stick with a super fund that's a chronic underperformer. Check out the best performers on page 111.

6. Know exactly what insurance and other benefits your super fund offers.

7. If you opt for a self managed super fund (SMSF), keep enough in your old fund to retain the insurance cover.

8. Make sure you consolidate your super funds into one fund. Go to www.superguru.com.au/grow-your-super/ consolidating-your-super/how-to-consolidate.

9. Get into salary sacrifice to turbo charge your super balance!

10. Slam money windfalls into your super to put your super balance on growth steroids!

11. Don't get caught ignoring these commandments!

POOJA'S STORY

"Finance matters can be complicated. Somebody you trust is very important."

When did you decide that you wanted to understand more about money?

When I was expecting my first child, life came more into focus and planning for the future became more real.

When did you get the idea that you wanted to buy a property?

I've always wanted to own a property. After getting married, it became a priority to get ready for having kids.

Has that been a good decision?

Yes, we're happy with the decision. Having a nice home for us and the kids, extra space and being close to schools are all great benefits.

What do you know about superannuation?

It's legislated that an employer has to contribute 9.5% of my pay to a chosen super fund, which will provide an income for me after a certain age.

Do you salary sacrifice? Why did you do this?

Yes, to increase my super and have extra money in retirement. It also helps reduce my taxable income.

What are your money goals? Do you and your partner/ husband i.e. Edward have the same goals?

My goals are to pay off our mortgage and set ourselves up for a comfortable retirement. Yes, we have common goals. We recently purchased a house and through the process of selling and buying a new place, we have a good idea of our expenses vs our income.

You're raising children now so a lot of your income would go there. But what are your future wealth accumulation goals?

We're trying to reduce our taxable income, do a renovation to increase the value of our property and focus on paying off our mortgage.

Are you a spendthrift or do you think about what you buy?

I frequently shop at Aldi and I'm always looking for the best value when we buy.

What else would you like to say?

We think the most important thing is to find a good financial adviser to help you manage your finances. Finance matters can be complicated. Somebody you trust is very important. In the past we didn't really gel with financial services that we used. Now we have a great tax accountant who has helped us in many ways and we're happy with their services.

11

TAX TIPS TO GET RICH

"I'm not evading tax in any way, shape or form. Of course, I'm minimising my tax. If anybody in this country doesn't minimise their tax, they want their head read. As a government I can tell you that you're not spending it that well that we should be paying extra tax."

Kerry Packer (1937-2005)

Too many people don't know the tax rules that we operate under here in Australia. This tax ignorance can cost you a lot of money. I've compiled a list of important tax questions you need to know the answers to. With the help of my tax buddy, David Giles, I intend to make you tax savvy enough to avoid losses and help make you money via the tax system.

Of course, evading tax or engaging in tax avoidance schemes is illegal. I believe we should all pay our fair share of tax because we live in a community and use services that our state and federal governments provide. Dodging tax and not contributing our fair share of tax (to assist those who need government support or services) isn't the right thing to do.

Equally it is incumbent on all of us to learn and to plan to be financially independent if we're capable of doing this. And guess what? That's why I wrote this book!

Q. Should I go to an accountant or tax agent?

A. Yes. You need to know what you don't know and paying for tax advice, which can be tax deductible, makes sense. If your life is simple, maybe a once-in-a-lifetime visit is enough. As your money life gets more complicated, these tax experts can be of priceless value.

Q. If I want to do my own tax, where should I start?

A. The Australian Tax Office (ATO) website has the usual deductions for various occupations and you can find them at www. ato.gov.au/Individuals/Income-and-deductions/Deductions-you-can-claim/Other-deductions/Deductions-for-specific-industries-and-occupations/ (Online lodgement is via my.gov.au. The ATO allows paper lodgment.

Q. Generally, what expenses for work are deductible?

A. If an expense is crucial to you earning income, then it's probably an allowable expense, though the Tax Office has ruled out some deductions. It's all about cause and effect with the ATO. If you can show the link, there's a deduction.

Q. Are my fares to work an allowable deduction?

A. As an employee "no" but as a contractor, pending the nature and frequency of the work, potentially. A contractor going into an office job and only working at a couple of places would not meet the criteria. However if they were working at many locations, you could argue that their home is the basis of work and when you step foot outside the home, you're on the job.

Q. What about my clothing?

A. Generally "no" but for contractors it could be "yes". The Tax Office has rulings on who can and can't make claims so it pays to get advice. Work uniforms are deductible to both employees and contractors (i.e. with a business logo) and occupational specific protective clothing will also be deductible. People get caught out claiming general clothing when there's nothing specific about the clothing to tie it to the occupation.

Q. Are training expenses to improve my chances of getting a promotion tax deductible?

A. Yes, as long as there's a formal qualification at the end, you can do this. A formal qualification can be as simple as a record of attendance. This is the ATO's official view:

- Maintain or improve the specific skills or knowledge you require in your current employment; or
- Result in, or is likely to result in, an increase in your income from your current employment.

You can't claim a deduction for self-education expenses for a course that doesn't have a sufficient connection to your current employment, even though it might be generally related to it, or enables you to get new employment.

Q. If I was a radio broadcaster and I paid for voice training, would that be deductible?

A. Yes. The nexus is created, as mentioned previously, it's called cause and effect.

Q. If my boss makes me use my car for going to jobs, are the car expenses deductible?

A. You can't claim the miles driving to work and home but if you logged the 'to jobs' driving while at work, you could claim these. You can claim either cents per kilometre up to 5,000 kilometres a year or complete a 12-week log book to claim a percentage.

Q. If I take work home and use a home office, are those related expenses claimable?

A. Yes, but the ATO will consider the need for the work to be completed at home. If there is a need, the ATO will offer methods of claiming: either the 'cents per hour' method or 'percentage area the home office occupies' option.

Q. If I decide to start a business, would the initial costs of talking to an accountant, a business planner, a lender, etc. be tax deductible?

A. Yes, these expenses from July 2015 have been deductible to small business on starting up. Deductible items include:

- in obtaining advice or services relating to the proposed structure or the proposed operation of the business; or
- in payment to an Australian government agency of a fee, tax or charge relating to setting up the business or establishing its operating structure. More information can be found on: www.ato.gov.au/forms/guide-to-depreciating-assest-2017/

Q. If the business was part-time, can I claim a proportion for the business calls, miles driven, etc.?

A. Yes but you'd need to keep good records. The expenses should be relatable to the income earned. If you made a profit of $20,000 and your telephone bill claimed was $30,000, there could be some questions asked by the ATO! The ATO uses benchmarks of similar business earning similar income to test if the expenses seem in keeping with the rest of the taxpayers industry.

Q. Is income-splitting legal for tax purposes?

A. The simple answer is "no" and that's when say a plumber "pretends" their spouse is a full-time worker in the business. This means the businesses income is split between the couple, reducing their tax bill. However, if the spouse ran the business and the plumber did the plumbing, then it could be a fair arrangement. The first example is illegal and is tax dodging according to the ATO, while the second example is quite legitimate.

Q. How is a sole trader or partnership taxed?

A. Income of the business is reduced by any related expenses and the leftover or net income is taxable, just like tax on a PAYE wage earner. A sole trader and partnership small business now get a $1,000 tax offset, which is a square up for the company tax cuts, that businesses that are companies have accessed.

Q. Is it tax-effective for a small business to set up as a company?

A. It can be, depending on the income of the business. The higher the income of the business, the more cost-effective the move to a company is. Because the company pays a company tax rate of 27.5% to 30%, it is a lot lower than the 45% top tax rate. The owners of a company can rearrange their income payments between wages, dividends and even loans that could reduce the overall tax bill for a certain time, which could help the business's cash flow. Accountants can offer legal ways to reduce the tax hit for a business when the structure of the operation is a company.

Other common examples would be for the directors to be paid a nominal wage and then the balance of the profits paid out in dividends into a family trust.

Q. Is getting a will drawn up by a solicitor tax deductible?

DO NOW

A. No. But you should still get a will done.

Q. Is a family trust a tax-effective vehicle? And who do they best suit? When would you ask an accountant or a solicitor the question: should I use a family trust?

A. A Family Trust can be an effective tax and asset protection vehicle that can be an integral part to long-term family planning. This structure best suits family investments generating an ongoing income or assets that have the potential to grow significantly over time. Any time a major family investment is considered, check with your advisers if a trust should be considered. Some people have grown a family business and when they came to sell it, their accountant has told them that their capital gains tax bill would have been smaller if the business was in a trust!

Q. What are some good ways to decrease my tax bill?

A. First, salary sacrifice is a good tax strategy. Here you can put up to $25,000 of your salary into super each year but this includes the 9.5% your boss puts into super for you. This money is taxed at 15% instead of your usual tax rate. (For more information on superannuation, check out chapter 10)

Q. What are the tax rates nowadays?

A. The table below shows Australian residents' tax rates 2018-19.

Taxable Income	Tax on this income
0- $18,200	Nil
$18,201- $37,000	19c for each $1 over $18,200
$37,001- $90,000	$3,572 plus 32.5c for each $1 over $37,000
$90,001- $180,000	$20,797 plus 37c for each $1 over $90,000
$180,000 and over	$54,097 plus 45c for each $1 over $180,000

Source: Australian Taxation Office

Also on top of those rates are the 2% Medicare Levy payable by all Australians, regardless of whether you have health insurance or not. The only exemptions are temporary foreign residents and those who earn less than $21,980 a year.

Q. Someone paying 37 cents in the dollar tax would save 22 cents in the dollar on the $25,000 they put into super through salary sacrifice — is that right?

A. Yes and because the Medicare Levy is based on taxable income, the reduction would be 24 cents in the dollar.
i.e. 37 cents + 2 cents - 15 cents = 24 cents saving. (For more on salary sacrifice see page 179)

Q. The more you earn, the more the tax saving through salary sacrifice? Is that right?

A. Yep. If you were only being taxed 19 cents in the dollar then the gain would be only 6 cents (19 cents + 2 cents -15 cents = 6 cents). But effective 1 July 2017, eligible individuals with an adjusted taxable income up to $37,697 will receive a LISTO (low income superannuation tax offset) payment to their super fund. The LISTO payment will be equal to 15% of their total concessional (pre-tax) super contributions for an income year, capped at $500. This means any tax paid by these low income Australians on their super contributions will be rebated and 'banked' back into their super funds.

Q. What is the spouse tax offset?

A. You can get a tax offset if you make a contribution to your spouse's or partner's super. The maximum offset is $540 and is available if you contribute $3,000 to their super and your spouse's income is under $37,000. It is called the Tax Offset for Spouse Contribution, and phases down to $0 if your partner's income exceeds $40,000. Income includes their assessable income plus any salary sacrifice contributions and any fringe benefits.

Q. What is the super co-contribution?

A. Super co-contributions help eligible people boost their retirement savings. If you're a low or middle-income earner and make personal (after-tax) contributions to your super fund, the government also makes a contribution (called a co-contribution) up to a maximum amount of $500.

There are two co-contribution income thresholds: a lower threshold ($37,696 for 2018–19) and a higher threshold ($52,697). If your total income is equal to or less than the lower threshold and you make personal contributions of $1,000 to your super account, you will receive the maximum co-contribution of $500. If your total income is between the two thresholds, your maximum entitlement will reduce progressively as your income rises. You will not receive any co-contribution if your income is equal to or greater than the higher threshold.

Q. If I earn a lot, am I slugged with more super tax?

A. Yes — have a look at this from the ATO: Previously, individuals with income and concessional super contributions greater than $300,000 triggered a Division 293 assessment. This meant for any income over $300,000 the related super contributions had an extra 15% tax on them.

Effective 1 July 2017, the government lowered the Division 293 income threshold to $250,000 for the 2017-18 and future financial years. An individual with income, and concessional super contributions, exceeding the $250,000 threshold will have an additional 15% tax imposed on the lesser of the excess over $250,000, or the concessional contributions (except excess contributions).

Q. What is PAYG and PAYE?

A. Pay as you go (PAYG) instalments is a system for making regular payments towards your expected annual income tax liability. It only applies to you if you earn business and/or investment income over a certain amount.

The Pay As You Earn (PAYE) system is a method of paying income tax. Your employer deducts tax and other government slugs, such as Medicare, super, etc. from your wages or occupational pension before paying you your wages or pension. Wages includes sick pay, maternity or paternity pay and adoption pay.

Q. Why is negative gearing seen as tax-effective?

A. Negative gearing can work with property and other assets, such as shares as well, and is more effective the higher the tax bracket you are in and the more tax you pay. In the property chapter I will go into more detail about negative gearing but suffice it to say that if you borrow money to buy an investment property, the interest becomes a cost and if the rent received is less than your interest bill and other costs such as the fees for real estate agents, lawyers, etc. and you make a loss, then this loss can be deducted from your other income earned in a financial year, which lowers your tax bill. This is why property investors who are negatively geared often get a nice refund. If you can work out your loss in advance, you can tell your paymaster and your regular tax bill can be reduced so you get your tax refund fortnightly or monthly depending on how often you're paid. (See chapter 9 on property).

Q. How do you access these tax refunds early?

A. Fill in a form called PAYG Withholding Variation E-Variation. Once submitted, the ATO will confirm the details and provide a letter to give to your paymaster.

OTHER LITTLE TAX 'TRICKS'

There are many things that a good accountant can show you. It can be good to get an accountant to look at your situation to see if they can see opportunities to legally claim deductions. Also a discussion with an accountant could show you 'stuff' that you could think about doing, which you wouldn't if you had not talked to an expert.

I used to have a part-time business when I was a teacher, coaching students economics. Many coaches took cash but I accepted cheques and turned the operation into Switzer Coaching School. I wanted to pay the right tax to avoid any ATO hassles. My accountant said because you have a part-time business where you drive to customers, you could lease a new car!

I had to work out what proportion of my driving was private and what proportion was business but it made the lease repayments much more affordable. It also made me look more successful. I have to say the whole relationship with the accountant taught my wife and I things that encouraged us to become a full-time business, as we got involved with the media. Knowledge opens the door to millions of possibilities!

In the early days I was reluctant to pay for help from experts. I thought I could do it all myself. If I have one regret it's that I wasn't as open to pay for expert advice as I should have been. Sometimes Australians can be 'tight' and not pay for advice that helps them prosper. These days I do this without feeling wallet pain.

I remember when I was speaking at an event years ago in Sydney. I'd written a book called *350 Ways to Grow Your Business.* The organisers suggested that I bring in the book to sell at the back of the room. I wasn't 100% comfortable with this but it was a large audience so the prospect of selling lots of books was high. And I'd convinced my wife to help! Before my session was finished, Maureen said that two men approached the table – one Aussie and one who was out here from South Africa. The Aussie thumbed through the book, at lightning speed reading as many tips as he could. The South African put his hand in his pocket and proceded to buy the book. Unashamedly, the Aussie said to him: "Mate, what are you doing? That book costs $29.95." His mate's response was: "I know. But it contains 350 ways to grow my business. And even if one of them works, I think it's worth the $30."

If you're reading this now, you've already paid the price so I'm not trying to sell to you. But I urge you to seek out good advice as you travel on your journey to financial independence. Overall, the investment you make will be worth every cent.

MY 11 TAX COMMANDMENTS

1. Understand that knowledge of tax can save as well as make you money. Paying for advice is one of the best investments you can make!

2. Find a good tax accountant/agent, who can help you put your tax life under a microscope. Ask friends who they use and would they recommend them. It's good if your accountant is a member of a professional association like CPA Australia, which binds them to a code of conduct.

3. Every time you think of something that may have a tax implication, write it down. Take your list to these meetings with your accountant so you can get answers for things you don't know.Use the page opposite to write down these questions.

4. Know all the legitimate tax deductions you're entitled to claim. I've listed a lot of them in this book!

5. Use potential tax deductions to improve your chances of a promotion (e.g. educational courses), your business and the building of your personal wealth.

6. Discover the tax benefits of investing in property.

7. Investigate the tax benefits around superannuation.

8. Understand the tax advantages of owning shares.

9. Never invest purely for tax deductions. Your main reason for investing is for income and capital gain.

10. Pay for advice to minimise your tax but remember we live in a community where services are provided by governments (e.g. education, health, roads, etc.) and we should all pay a fair amount of tax.

11. Keep these commandments!

QUESTIONS TO ASK YOUR ACCOUNTANT

1. I have compiled a list of questions I'd like answers to. Can we start our meeting this way?

2. ....

   ....

3. ....

   ....

4. ....

   ....

5. ....

   ....

6. ....

   ....

7. ....

   ....

WRITE DOWN — Take this with you to your next meeting. It will show your accountant how serious you are!

12 107 MONEY TIPS TO MAKE YOU RICHER

---

*"I don't apologise for my diamonds, Rolls
Royce, Range Rover, or anything. Look,
Queen Elizabeth has more diamonds than me.
Why don't people criticise her?"*

Kimora Lee Simmons, US model.

In this chapter. I'm offering you 107 tips that I've collected while writing this book. Some of these are general money tips for beginners but everyone could benefit from revisiting these chestnuts. Sometimes we forget the simple start out messages. I've then grouped the next sets of tips about investing in the share market, superannuation and property categories.

Finally, I've provided tips for those who have built up knowledge and wealth over time. This is what I want for everyone who reads this book. Build up your wealth and keep learning. Learning is a life-long process. Down the track, I want you to be a sophisticated investor and have the comforts and peace of mind that go with a financially secure life.

BEGINNERS' TIPS

1. Start early. Use discipline and build up a reserve of money.

2. Allocate a portion of income to saving that you can later use for an investment.

3. Put away 3-5% of your income as a bare minimum in the early days. Aim to save 15% of your income for 40 years!

4. It's good to have a definite plan but any commitment to any saving is better than nothing.

5. Review your plan at least once a year. Have it in front of you always.

6. Work out your lifestyle to create savings. For example, buy Pay TV services to avoid going to the movies and hiring videos could save you more. This shows the value of a plan.

7. Use credit cards to YOUR advantage.

8. Check out the fees you pay on your mobile phones, any loans you have, superannuation fees and charges, insurance, banking, etc. Try to cut them down.

9. Avoid department store credit cards.

10. There are expensive and cheaper credit cards. Do your homework, read the fine print and swap.
Go to www.ratecity.com.au/credit-cards.

11. If you're looking for money to save, make sure you do a budget.

12. Cutting lifestyle costs saves you much more than you think.

13. Smart banking can save you lots. Make sure you have low fee accounts.

14. When leasing, ask to see what the total cost will be so you can compare it against borrowing and buying.

15. Invest in yourself, as education can create income

opportunities. Career or money education can be rewarding.

16. Don't procrastinate when income circumstances change for the worst. Treat it like an "intensive care ward" and set things right quickly. This could mean changing your spending patterns, renegotiating loans and talking to lenders.

17. Don't over-insure or under-insure. Check out your insurance coverage, its cost and compare alternatives.

18. Find out what tax-saving opportunities exist for someone like you. Let an accountant look at your circumstances to see if tax can be legally reduced. The cost is tax deductible!

19. Borrowing sensibly can create wealth.

20. Understand your cashflow when locking into an investment deal that involves borrowing and repayments.

21. Don't go overboard on the advertised payoff from negative gearing. You can lose.

22. Positive gearing is OK too. You pay tax but you're also earning income.

23. Invest for the long term. Looking at the All Ords between 1959 and 1989, the trend return on average was 6.7%. Between 1984 and 1999 it worked out around 14%. And between 1974 and 1999 it was 13.8%. But over the long term, shares go up 10% per annum over a decade where half the return comes from dividends.

24. Don't invest in one asset type, such as all shares or all property.

25. Smart investing information can be found at ASIC's website called MoneySmart at www.moneysmart.gov.au/investing/invest-smarter

26. If you have too many credit card debts, talk to your lender about debt consolidation, which should deliver you a lower interest rate.

SHARE MARKET TIPS

27. Don't just hold Australian shares. Some overseas shares give you diversification.

28. A slump in the stock market can KO a one-time good share where it loses 75% of its value. It could take 8 years for it to recover.

29. Many advisers recommend buying or selling in blocks or parts of share holdings. This means if you thought the market had hit a top but if you had nagging doubts, then a partial sale followed by a wait-and-see period could be the sensible way to go.

30. You should learn about the signs in a market that encourage you to buy or sell.

31. While unit trusts or a managed fund are less vulnerable to a sell than an individual share, they can cop a terrible hiding in a big sell down of the market.

32. Even if you're planning to be a passive investor locked into a fund, educate yourself about what fund managers do, how trustworthy investor information is, what your downside risks are and whether you can cope with a bad run for the market.

33. Here's great advice from one of the best and richest investors — Warren Buffet. He says there should be no difference in your approach to buying shares than there should be if you're planning to buy the business outright. Like buying anything, you should do your homework, asking

what is the price? Is it good value? Will it be good value in the future? The more work you do, the more likely it is that you will avoid a dumb decision.

34. Some market players swear by the investment clock, though at some odd times they have sworn at the investment predictor! (See below for my explanation).

THE INVESTMENT CLOCK

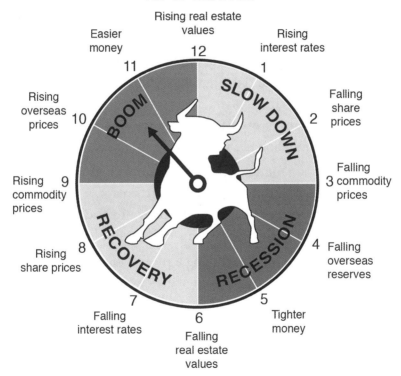

Source: Bourse Communications

The investment clock above begs the questions: What time is it? Basically, during a prolonged investment cycle, money flows from the stock market to real estate to interest-paying securities and back to the stock market. The movement of interest rates is a critical cause for the popularity of shares, property or fixed interest products.

A simple summary could be that as interest rates rise, shares become less attractive and rising interest rates eventually hurt an economy, sometimes causing a recession. Share prices fall before a recession. After a share market crash, there's often a flight to quality and real estate prices rise. But eventually, high interest rates will choke off the property price boom and that's when it might be sensible to lock your money into high interest rate accounts. When interest rates fall, it then would be wise to chase shares again. This is a tricky asset chase and the development can be uneven and you can look as though you've moved too early. In some cases you might have. If it was easy, we'd all be millionaires and being a millionaire wouldn't mean much!

35. If you're not a market expert or amateur stock market 'guru', invest for the long term — 5-10 years — and don't have a heart attack looking at the daily ups and downs of the share prices and the price of units in funds.

36. No-one ever went broke taking a profit. Sometimes it's a good idea to sell some of your shares when they go for a big rise to pocket some profit, in case the good news is totally reversed.

37. You have to understand franking or tax credits on dividends.

38. If you plan to run your portfolio of shares, a number between 10-20 different stocks is recommended. Make sure they aren't similar stocks, for example, all banking shares.

39. Don't simply believe generalizations based on the history of stock markets but use them to construct your action plan.

40. If you can't do your own homework on shares then a managed fund could be your best way to access the benefits of the stock market.

41. When do you buy shares or a managed fund? A couple of years after a stock market crash has a good history to tell.

42. When do I get out of a bull market? That's hard. Bull markets run for about 10 years but the longest went for 15 years and since 1960 there have been two that lasted for over 12 years.

43. Experts also know to never take rules of thumb as gospel. Undoubtedly, many fund managers look at these regular historical occurrences/stats to help their call when to get in or get out. There are far more technical ones but I reckon they all help.

44. What if you miss the chance to sell? Well, some experts say to get rid of the companies that look 'suss' and keep the good, rock-solid ones and in fact you could even buy shares in these at vastly lower prices.

45. But what if I could never see myself buying and selling shares but could see myself relying on superannuation and other investment fund products? If that's you, get used to going to www.superatings.com.au, www.chantwest. com.au and www.morningstar.com.au to find out the best performing funds and then check out the fees they charge and compare them against others.

46. Check these funds' performances over 3, 5 and 10 years if possible.

47. One appeal of shares over real estate is that you can buy smaller amounts of shares and you don't have to deal with tenants, who could trash your asset.

48. Shares on average over the past 50 years have returned 5-8% over and above inflation. (This doesn't mean every share has achieved this.)

49. Picking the timing for a stock market is difficult and you can still make good money over a 10-year period buying into an expensive market. However, taking a 10-year position on a well-diversified portfolio bought after a significant stock market fall makes good investment sense.

50. If you're buying shares only in Australia, then you might have too many of your eggs in one basket. This is a case for having some international shares.

51. Good quality under-valued shares are often good value. A panic-stricken stock market can often over-sell good shares.

52. A tax benefit can be a silly reason for an investment.

53. Only use surplus money for speculation in shares.

54. You should be fully aware of the tax advantages open to you as an investor. Do your homework or talk to an accountant or financial planner.

55. Regularly look to online broker websites such as nabtrade to get up-to-date market info and insights.

56. A stockbroker's advice can be good or bad, but remember it is your money you are investing so it should be your choice. As Rupert Murdoch once said: "The buck stops with the guy who signs the cheques." (Cheques aren't so popular nowadays but I guess you get the message.)

57. Shares sold off when stock markets are crashing can bounce back to more accurate valuation levels in a short space of time. This is why some experts recommend you invest for the long term in good quality companies or products. And

sometimes the best time to buy quality stocks that pay good dividends is when there's a big market sell off and good stocks' prices fall along with bad stocks. Contrarian investors often pick up great bargains that make them rich in the long run!

58. There are two reasons why people don't get rich — they work hard instead of working smart and they don't curtail their spending enough to acquire the savings to invest.

SUPERANNUATION TIPS

59. For a satisfactory retirement someone needs to put 12% into superannuation for 30 years.

60. For a better than satisfactory retirement, ASFA says to put 15% of income into superannuation for 40 years. This should give you a retirement income of about 60% of your pre-retirement annual income.

61. Take advantage of government super incentives, such as the Co-Contribution, Tax Offset for Spouse Contributions.(See page 185)

62. A good performing fund today could be a poor performer tomorrow, so monitor your fund and don't be afraid to switch. On the other hand, don't be too quick to leave a fund because of one bad year following a number of good ones.

63. If you're in business for yourself, starting your own super fund for investments can be very tax effective and profitable, especially if you want to buy a shop or factory.

64. If your super balances are uneven, split super contributions with your spouse or partner. In the long term, this may help protect you and your partner from Government changes to

super. (See page 185)

65. If you want to give your super a "sugar hit", don't forget about the "bring forward rule" that allows you to make 3 year's of contributions in one hit.

PROPERTY TIPS

66. Buy the worst house in the best street.

67. One advantage of real estate over shares is that if the market turns against you, you can always live in your house or unit.

68. There are those who argue that renting can be more economically advantageous than buying a home but it does require that the money leftover from renting instead of buying is invested profitably.

69. If you can't afford to buy a house you can live in, then you could become a landlord owning a house in an area where you want to live in the future. There are tax advantages of doing this and when your wage rises, you could move into that property.

70. Property 'princess' Margaret Lomas says you don't have to buy an investment property near where you live. Buy anywhere where tenants really want to live and capital gain will follow.

71. Never buy a property on a battle-axe block. This is a block of land behind another, with access from the street through.

72. Take care you don't over-capitalise your real estate assets when you renovate.

73. When recession talk turns into recession reality and unemployment rises there are generally good buying

opportunities in real estate, so don't worry about FOMO — fear of missing out when house price rises become crazy in a property boom.

74. If you buy a home to live in, paying off the mortgage quickly is seen by many money experts as a very tax effective way to go.

75. Some people collect a pile of properties by using the capital gain on one property to get a new loan to buy another property. That said, you need to be able to service the loans so make sure you can stand a 3-4% interest rate rise and your job or business income is safe. Fixing your interest rate can give you more certainty but when the fixed term ends you could be in a higher interest rate environment.

76. Don't panic if you take out a relatively expensive loan for property as you can always pay to end it and eventually the savings from a low cost loan will make the switch worthwhile. The break cost can be high but a low rate loan might make it worthwhile.

77. Mortgage offset accounts with unlimited drawback are a good way to reduce your mortgage.

78. When looking for loans, use those groups that survey a whole list of lenders and then compare their recommendations to the lowest cost lenders. Make sure they offer the conditions you might need, such as unlimited drawback facilities. The following websites are worth a look:
www.ratecity.com.au
www.finder.com.au
www.mozo.com.au

79. For an investment property, many experts recommend an interest only loan and if interest rates are more likely to rise

than fall, they swing towards a fixed rate of interest.

80. Sometimes you do have to think outside the square to create the circumstances to be different. Being rich is a minority thing and not being rich is a majority thing.

TIPS FOR THE MORE SOPHISTICATED INVESTOR

81. Never invest in something you don't understand.

82. Be careful when it comes to tax shelters.

83. When it comes to primary production, film or overseas schemes, talk to the Australian Tax Office (ATO) and the Australian Securities and Investments Commission (ASIC). Generally I'd steer clear of anything that offers high returns because they come with high risks.

84. There is a list of commonly overlooked tax deductions — make sure you're not missing out on claiming them. They include fees for preparing your tax, home office expenses, interest paid to the ATO, depreciation on buildings used for investment, borrowing costs for finance, meal and accommodation when travelling, depreciation for home computers, and more. Do your homework and check out the Tax Office website: www.ato.gov.au/Individuals/Income-and-deductions/Deductions-you-can-claim/

85. Treat your wealth building programme like a business. Make a plan. Write it down and review it regularly. Change it as circumstances require.

86. Meaure your investment results at least once a quarter.

87. Don't be afraid to use professionals to make better investment decisions.

88. Build a support team, which might include a financial

adviser, accountant, stockbroker, lawyer, possibly a psychiatrist and www.switzer.com.au!

89. Read quality newspapers, magazines and websites to be across important developments that could affect your investment decisions.

90. Read the fine print on all big transactions and understand it, as this will give you an edge. It will also minimize the chances of paying more than you should and ignoring potential benefits. (Start with your bank accounts, credit cards and loyalty/frequent flyer programmes.)

91. Look for associations that represent your interests such as the Australian Shareholders Association, the SMSF Association, etc.

92. Also contact the Australian Securities and Investments Commission (ASIC), the Australian Stock Exchange (ASX) and the Australian Consumers Association (CHOICE) and use their websites to get money-wise.

93. Don't be afraid to go to two or three financial advisers until you find the one you feel comfortable with. Or teach yourself to be your own adviser.

94. Don't be afraid to copy the lead of very successful investors and fund managers, though remember they don't always get it right.

95. Sign up for investing newsletters and websites that give you stock selection ideas such as *The Switzer Report*.

96. When you go to a financial adviser, make sure you know exactly what you'll be charged and what your total cost of doing business will be. If you're paying more than 1%, you better be getting annual returns better than average returns.

97. Borrowing or gearing can be very profitable but make sure you fully understand the risk or downside.

98. Be careful when using margin loans for buying shares because you could be asked to pay a margin call or extra money if the value of the shares falls too far.

99. Be wary of products sold to you where the salesperson picks up a commission.

100. Even if you're investing for the long term, regularly review your investments or portfolio.

101. Always know and be prepared for the worst-case scenario and make sure you can always service your debts.

102. Come along to our investor days (www.switzerevents.com.au). You will be surprised how much you learn.

103. Watch Switzer TV on YouTube (www.youtube.com/switzermedia).

104. Subscribe to SwitzerDaily (www.switzer.com.au) it's free!

105. Be commited to life long learning.

106. When you have the means, give back to others.

107. And remember if something's worth doing, it's worth doing for money.

These tips and indeed this whole book is aimed at you learning how to make money, not waste it. This is my message to you. It's up to you to do the work that will involve continuous lifelong learning. I urge you to keep walking down the path of financial freedom. Once on that path, you will never want to go anywhere but forward.

"A journey of a thousand miles must begin with a single step."

Lao Tsu, Chinese philosopher, born 601 BC

13 ONE-PAGE FINANCIAL PLAN

"The greatest obstacle to your success is you. The reality is that it all comes down to changing the way you think."

Peter Switzer, and every other motivational speaker the world has ever seen!

I know most people want a shortcut to economic heaven where the inhabitants are rolling in money. I was recently reminded of this and how we want fast answers to complex matters when I saw a friend carrying a book titled *Buddhism for Busy People!*

What follows is a "Busy Person's Guide to Getting Rich". You could call this a 1-page plan (even though it's across two pages) or a 7-step blueprint for getting rich.

Let's kick this off.

A BUSY PERSON'S GUIDE TO GETTING RICH

1. Write down what you want in life, such as a home, a car, a great job and plenty of spare cash so you can help yourself and the people you care about. These are your goals.

2. You have to create your personal balance sheet. I've drawn up one for you over the page. Stay with me on this, as I'm going to make this understandable. [WRITE DOWN] A balance sheet shows your assets i.e. stuff you own that has value, from cash to cars to jewellery and so on. You then add up your debts and take this from your assets and you end up with your equity, or what you're really worth in dollar terms.

3. Work out what you spend each week and what you spend it on. This is contained in a budget but let's call it a "where your money goes" checklist. (You can can fill one in on page 42)

4. Try and GST your life by cutting your spending by 10%. If you spend $50,000 a year, your personal GST gives you $5,000 to invest. One less cup of coffee a day could save you $25 a week or $1,300 a year. It's that simple.

5. If you took this $1,300 a year and put it in your super fund at 8% for 30 years, it would give you $78,000. But if you do this for 45 years, it turns into $173,000. And that's adjusted for inflation. So in 45 years you'd be able to buy the same stuff as you could today. And that's because you gave up just one coffee a day!

6. If you want to have access to the money that you've saved, you could invest it in an exchange traded fund, such as IOZ (see page 77 for more details) which gives you an investment in Australia's top 200 companies. On any day, if the stock market

rose by 2%, you'd be 2% richer. History shows that the stock market rises by 10% a year on average over a 10-year period. This chart shows what I want for you. Between 1970 and 2019, that $10,000 rolled into $970,048 and it can happen by automatic pilot by simply letting the money snowball in something like an ETF, such as IOZ. If you follow the black line on the chart below, it shows how the $10,000 ended up being $423,439 by 2009, one year after the GFC KO'd the stock market by 50%. And by 2019, it grew to $970,048.

MY FAVOURITE CHART: 31 DECEMBER 1969 - 30 APRIL 2019
Total returns for a $10,000 investment with no acquisition costs or taxes and all income reinvested

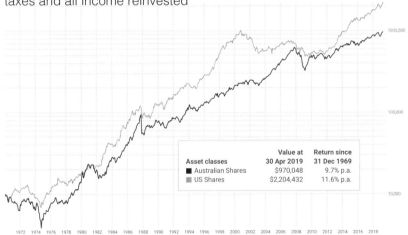

Asset classes	Value at 30 Apr 2019	Return since 31 Dec 1969
■ Australian Shares	$970,048	9.7% p.a.
■ US Shares	$2,204,432	11.6% p.a.

Source: Andex Charts Pty Ltd/ Vanguard Investments Australia Ltd.

7. Try to be patient and buy great quality assets —properties, shares, etc. — when everyone is negative and gloomy. As the world's greatest investor, Warren Buffett advises: "Be fearful when others are greedy and greedy when others are fearful."

If you adopt my 7 steps guide to getting rich, you'll get rich over the long term. May the riches be with you...

YOUR PERSONAL BALANCE SHEET

What you own	$	Your debts	$
1.		1.	
2.		2.	
3.		3.	
4.		4.	
5.		5.	
6.		6.	
7.		7.	
8.		8.	
9.		9.	
10.		10.	
(1) Total		**(2) Total**	

Now do the maths...

Your Net Worth 1- 2 = ...

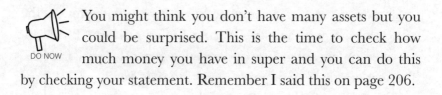

You might think you don't have many assets but you could be surprised. This is the time to check how much money you have in super and you can do this by checking your statement. Remember I said this on page 206.

PETER SWITZER'S MONEY HITS

I've always found music and songs inspirational. Who doesn't feel lifted by the theme from the movie Chariots of Fire? Or Queen's We Are The Champions? Or Born in the USA by the boss, Bruce Springstein? All these songs take many of us to a higher level. I hope my playlist below takes you to a higher, richer level!

PETER'S MONEY MIXTAPE

© Peter Switzer 2019
To be played whenever you
feel in a money state of mind!

A

1. Money, Pink Floyd

2. Money, Money, Money, ABBA

3. Money for Nothing, Dire Straits

4. Money Too Tight to Mention, Simply Red

5. Money, That's What I Want, The Beatles

6. Rich Girl, Hall & Oates

7. She Works Hard for the Money, Donna Summer

8. Can't Buy Me Love, The Beatles

GLOSSARY

All Ordinaries Index/ All Ords (AOI): The All Ordinaries is the oldest share index in Australia. A market capitalisation style index, it is based on the share prices of the 500 largest companies listed on the Australian Securities Exchange (ASX).

ASX/Australian Securities Exchange: is the primary exchange for Australian stocks based in Sydney.

ASX 200 (also S&P/ASX 200): is a benchmark share index that consists of the 200 largest companies by market capitalisation listed on the ASX. S&P Dow Jones (S&P) maintains the index.

Bear Market: is a market in which share prices are falling, by more than 20%, encouraging selling.

Bull Market: is a market in which share prices are rising, encouraging buying.

Capital Gain: is the rise in the value of an asset such as shares or an investment property. When the asset is sold and the gain is realised, it becomes liable for capital gains tax (CGT).

Concessional contributions: super contributions made by your employer (the compulsory 9.5%), by salary sacrifice, or where a tax deduction is claimed. Subject to a yearly cap of $25,000. Called "concessional" because the contributions are a tax deductible expense for the entity making the contributions.

Dividends: a payment made by a company to its shareholders, usually as a distribution of profits.

Dow Jones: the oldest share index in the USA, it is a simple arithmetic index of 30 of the largest companies. Most of these companies are household names.

Exchange traded fund (ETF): is a managed fund that can be bought or sold on an exchange like the ASX. Many ETFs are low cost funds that passively track an index such as the ASX 200 by replicating the stocks that make up that index.

GST: a value-added tax levied on most goods and services at a rate of 10%. Paid to the Federal Government by businesses, it is then fully shared with the States and Territories. Businesses only remit the net GST they collect, after deducting the GST they pay for their purchases of goods and services.

Liquidation: is a situation in which an asset is sold in order to get cash, usually with some urgency.

Managed fund: a unit trust where your money is pooled together with other investors. An investment manager then invests those monies in shares, property or other assets. You own units in the trust, and may receive periodic distributions of income.

Margin Loan: a loan taken out to invest in shares or managed funds. The shares are the security for the loan. If the market tanks, you might be required to address a "margin call" and provide additional security. Margin loans can help you increase your returns, but they can also magnify your losses and are only suitable for experienced investors.

NASDAQ: a US stock exchange that tends to attract technology, biotechnology and other "new age" companies. Facebook, Alphabet, Apple, Amazon and Netflix are listed on the NASDAQ. The index of the top 100 companies on this exchange is referred to as the "NASDAQ100" or "NASDAQ" for short.

Negative gearing: where you use borrowed money to purchase an asset such as an investment property, and the expenses including interest exceed the income from the asset. The net loss is then claimed as a tax deduction to offset tax payable on other income such as your salary. With positive gearing, there is no net investment loss.

Non-concessional contributions: a personal contribution to super for which no tax deduction is available (i.e. from your own after tax monies). Subject to an annual cap of $100,000. Called "non-concessional" because the contributions are not tax deductible.

Pension: a periodic payment by the Federal Government to a retiree (aged pension), or person with a disability (disability support pension). Superannuation funds also pay pensions to their retired members, with the member usually nominating the amount that is paid. In the case of super pensions, the government stipulates a minimum annual payment based on the member's age and their super balance.

S&P 500: a benchmark share index for determining the overall health of the U.S. stock market. It consists of the 500 largest US companies by market capitalisation.

Salary sacrifice: in lieu of salary, you direct your employer to make an additional contribution to super. The benefit to you is that this is done "before tax" rather than "after tax" – so more money goes into the super fund. Salary sacrifice contributions, together with the employer's compulsory 9.5%, are counted against your concessional cap of $25,000 pa.

Self-managed super fund (SMSF): a do-it-yourself superannuation scheme designed for those who want direct control over their retirement savings and investments. A SMSF can have up to four members, all of whom are trustees of the fund or directors of the company that acts as the fund's trustee.

Shares/ Stocks: the ownership of a company is divided into shares. Companies list their shares on exchanges such as the ASX where they can be readily traded, forming a share market. Shares are also called stocks (e.g. stock market is another term for a share market).

Superannuation: a compulsory savings system designed to provide income support in retirement. By law, employers contribute 9.5% of an employee's wages into super. When the employee retires or turns 65, they can withdraw the money, either through a lump sum or through the payment of a regular pension.

Tax offset: Tax offsets, sometimes referred to as rebates, directly reduce the amount of tax payable on your taxable income

"Every day, think as you wake up, today I am fortunate to be alive. I have a precious human life. I am not going to waste it."

The Dalai Lama.